Student Book

SRA

Corrective Reading

Decoding Strategies

Decoding B1

Siegfried Engelmann

Linda Carnine

Gary Johnson

Linda Meyer

Wesley Becker

Julie Eisele

Cover Photo: BlueMoon Stock/SuperStock

MHEonline.com

Copyright © McGraw-Hill Education

All rights reserved. No part of this publication may be reproduced or distributed in any form or by any means, or stored in a database or retrieval system, without the prior written consent of McGraw-Hill Education, including, but not limited to, network storage or transmission, or broadcast for distance learning.

Send all inquiries to:
McGraw-Hill Education
8787 Orion Place
Columbus, OH 43240

ISBN: 978-0-07-611215-9
MHID: 0-07-611215-2

Printed in the United States of America.

20 QVS 19 18

Contents

Lesson 1

1 m f l s n

2 j k t d p

3 can sack cat clap stick pack

4 (a) did land man keep sits lip

(b) seeds man sand keep last fill

(c) keep lip jam last sits did

5 the that this teeth

6 this teeth the that

7 can sack cat clap stick pack

8 sack can pack stick cat clap

9

1. The cat can sleep in a lap.
2. Did that man see the last plan?
3. Slip this stick in the pack.
4. Keep the pan in that sack.
5. Did the stick land in sand?

Lesson 2

1

l s m f n

2

p d k j t

3

cap lack trick clip slack

4

(a) and this plant math seeds

(b) plant did feeds than pick

(c) ant than sticks did fits

(d) pack dad teeth this stick

(e) this teeth fits seeds lamps

(f) can this sticks plant lamps

(g) seeds cap did math than

5

1. This cap fits in that pack.
2. Did that tack stick the cat?
3. Plant the seed in sand.
4. Clip that last plant and keep a tip.
5. Dad can see a cat that sleeps.
6. This ant sits in a sack.

Lesson 3

1

m d f j n

p l s k t

2

a e i ee

3

r w g h

4

(a) run will deer truck flag

(b) milk had sun go she

(c) ship black so he trip

(d) sun cash store slip corn

(e) fast mud we sheet hill

(f) so wish for jump black

5

1. Can she go in a store?
2. Will that truck slip in mud?
3. At last she has a black cat.
4. We had no plan for a trip.
5. That truck can go so fast.

Lesson 4

1

n f d j m

s l k t p

2

e i ee a

3

h w g r

4

(a) no three sink cup fits corn

(b) than drug meet go us store

(c) fun so wish sleep will torn

(d) sink for drug three than sheep

(e) math us drink torn fish go

(f) corn with junk so sheet flag

5

1. Three sheep sleep with a deer.
2. I will fill this gas can.
3. That store has junk in it.
4. Will that milk last us for a week?
5. Can we go in the drug store?
6. I need a pack for the trip.

Lesson 5

1

d l t s m f

n g h r w

2

o e a i u ee

3

ol old told colt gold cold

4

(a) got wish cold free hand sheets

(b) shot track milk fold sleep truck

(c) seems win that told flag rock

(d) ship on plan move gold drip

(e) colt wish stop free store old

(f) teeth for drip old rash shop

5

to do

6

1. We will go for more fish at the store.
2. Stick with me and we will have fun.
3. She sat with me at the track meet.
4. She had a fun trip.
5. Is he free to go with us?
6. If this is the last meet, we will go.
7. The junk did not fit in that truck.

Lesson 6

1

d n f l s n

r m g w h

2

a i e u ee

3

ol old sold fold told

4

(a) shop drip path green got

(b) three grass win flap cop duck

(c) wish told hand store steep ship

(d) cash more with rock seems that

(e) got duck path cold green for

(f) flap green sold on with more

(g) drip sod track store seems path

5

was said do to

6

1. The man told him, “Hop in this truck.”
2. She said, “Fill this sack with fish.”

7

1. A steep hill had green grass on it.
2. If that truck can not stop, it will hit a tree.
3. Can three sheep sleep on rocks?
4. His feet feel sore and cold.
5. Fold that green rag and hand it to me.
6. Will we slip in the street?
7. Will Pat feed a cat?

Lesson 7

1

w h t ck

r f s d n

2

e a i u ee

3

ch chip much inch chop cheer chill

4

b hub bill be rob back

bed crab bad bust

5

ing sing ring bring selling camping

sending lifting filling meeting

6

(a) fold send hand clock much

(b) pole inch camping greet got sung

(c) sunk horse fond send trunk

(d) more store dent cheer list

(e) then chop bust meeting cold

(f) slap now when them rang

7

have give was to said do

8

1. She said, "How much can we send?"
2. He said, "I keep lots of junk in that trunk."

9

1. He told them, "See me at the meeting."
2. The man has more cats than I have.
3. Will she be selling that horse this week?
4. If we can do it, we will go camping.
5. How did she do in the math class?
6. She said, "Fold up that sheet and hand it to me."
7. How much sand will he give us?

Lesson 8

1

w ck h t r

s d f n

2

a u ee i

3

(a) th sh ch wh

(b) which such whip much

wheel when chip shop

4

b rub rob bill bob bed bad crab back

5

ing ring bring meeting sending feeling filling

6

of you have give do said was to

7

(a) when bed cold shop list think

(b) form sending how class rub no

(c) dent much next trip gold then ring

(d) tell track list feeling bad wish

(e) bring got truck cash next wish

8

1. Is she sending me to the meeting?
2. Tell them how well you ran at the track meet.
3. Hold the gold, and do not drop it.
4. Do you need a lot more cash for this trip?
5. How can we shop if we do not have the list?
6. His truck has a bad dent in the top.
7. When we get back, I will go for a run.
8. Will the cold bring more sun?

Lesson 9

1

o e

th wh ch sh ing

b i r d a

2

e she met send

week be bell spend

3

er her letter sister

after clerk were

rancher better

4

ing ring bringing going

doing singing sending morning

5

faster last path fishing sell bus

morning bring horse which were

ranch think much when

6

they give was have of

woman said you what

7

(a) which trucker person bring path her

(b) sore when sending more ranch bus

(c) sister going last horse math met

(d) person were think much bed last

(e) rancher fishing doing selling better lifts

8

1. The woman in the black hat sings with us.
2. Last week we had to sell the truck.
3. That woman was the last person on the bus.
4. He said, "I did not think we had to do more math."
5. Which letter did you send her?
6. They were not singing when the bus got back.
7. Bring them back to class in the morning.
8. What were you doing when the bell rang?
9. When will we win a track meet?

Lesson 10

1

o e

wh th ch ing sh

d a r b i

2

e we bell red best

feed be next fed went

3

er better clerk letter

were seller her sister

after batter person

4

ing sing sending morning

going doing ringing bringing

5

sleeping chips streets cash last

bets faster bring dress cow

were deep order sweep much

path next fishing help think

6

show blow low snow flowing

7

middle question have they

what was you woman

8

(a) sending better sweep path order

(b) bringing thank letter were shelf

(c) next bringing streets dress much

(d) fills person morning last sleeping

(e) best faster doing bets her

9

1. Were they with you when you met her?
2. The snow in the streets was deep.
3. I can drink as much milk as you can.
4. She said, "Let me show you how to fold a sheet."
5. That woman went for a run this morning.
6. Were you in the street after the truck crash?
7. What did that man tell you to do?
8. After his nap, he will feel much better.
9. Bring me the dress with the spot on it.
10. Which path do you think is the best?

Lesson 11

1

o e ten pond we how

teen got tell wet mom

so seem get lot down

2

lift order which shelf rancher creek

over back sweep trash path brown

fell horse going back told black

3

A	B	C
plan	shop	rub
planning	shopping	rubbing
planned	shopped	rubbed

4

know my into question

middle what you they

woman do person

5

(a) lift shopping which black wet

(b) creek got planning jump over

(c) trash milk sister sweep brown

(d) horse path rubbed rancher going

(e) get thank person down teen

6 Tim Asked Questions

Tim asked a lot of questions. His dad told him to go to the store for milk. Tim asked, "Which store?"

When his mom told him to set the cups on the shelf, he asked, "Which shelf?"

His sister said, "Give me a hand."

Tim said, "Which hand?"

Last week, Tim was at a ranch. The rancher told him, "Get on a horse and go down that path."

Tim asked 2 questions. What questions do you think he asked?

[1]

The rancher told Tim to get on a black horse, and Tim did that. Then Tim went down the path and got to a creek.

He said, "How is this horse going to get over this creek?"

The horse showed him how. The horse jumped over the creek. But Tim fell into the creek when the horse jumped.

Tim sat in the middle of the creek and said to the horse, "I see how you got over the creek."

Then he asked a question. What do you think he asked?

[2]

Lesson 12

1

oo too broom soon room

2

began before begin

3

orders pals next lift sweeping

were they back mad

trash help set think just

4

A	B	C
stopping	robber	hopping
runner	sitting	robbed
grinned	dropped	stopper

5

one where there gave day

what know my you give into

6

(a) think were sweeping locked just

(b) trash orders next lift asked

(c) mad helped dropping they began

(d) pals begin set stopping orders

(e) give runner robbed next were

7 Tim and His Big Sister

Tim's big sister did not ask questions. She gave orders. She told her dog what to do. She told her pals what to do. But when she told Tim what to do, he asked questions.

One day she said, "Get a broom and sweep the room."

Then Tim asked, "Which broom and which room?"

His sister said, "The red broom. Get that broom. Then sweep this room."

Tim said, "Where is the red broom?"

His sister said, "It is next to the brown broom."

Do you know what Tim asked next?

Tim's sister said, "The brown broom is in the back room."

[1]

Tim got the broom and began to sweep. Just then, his sister yelled, "Help me lift this trash can."

Tim asked, "How can I keep on sweeping and lift trash cans?"

His sister yelled, "Drop that red broom and help me."

Tim set the broom down and went to the trash can. He asked, "What is in that trash can?"

His sister got mad. She said, "What do you think is in the trash can?"

Tim said, "That is my question. If you ask questions, I will give orders."

He did just that. He told his sister what to do.

[2]

Lesson 13

1

oo room soon broom

2

A	B	C
sitting	planner	grinned
clapped	filled	slipper
dripping	slamming	sitter

3

cold morning mom socks green Ron's cop

slacks just robbers need dogs sister shells

shelf were glad freeze lumps legs person

4

A	B	C
save	like	hope
saving	liking	hoping
saved	liked	hoped

5

are my who one

what before where

there began day

happened asked

town down gave

6

(a) green hope shelf planned going

(b) slacks dogs lumps liking need

(c) clapped socks freeze mom robbers

(d) legs save cold sister just

(e) morning person glad were sitting

7

Ron's Socks

On a cold morning, Ron went to his mom and said, "I have no socks."

His mom said, "You have lots and lots of socks. You have red socks for running and socks that go with black slacks."

"No, Mom," Ron said. "I do not have one sock in my room."

Ron's mom said, "If sock robbing is going on, I will get a cop."

She did just that. A cop went in Ron's room and said, "There are no socks in this room. There must be sock robbers in this town." Then the cop said, "I will get more cops." Soon, there were 18 cops in Ron's room.

[1]

One cop said, "We need dogs to track down the sock robbers."

Just then, Ron's little sister asked, "What are cops doing in this room?" Ron told her what happened.

Ron's little sister grinned and said, "Sock robbers did not get the socks. I got the socks to hold the shells that were on my shelf."

The 18 cops were not mad. They were glad that they did not have to get dogs and track the sock robbers.

But Ron's mom was not glad. She told Ron's little sister, "Give Ron back his socks before his feet freeze."

His sister did that. Then she filled her socks with shells. Now she has big lumps on her legs.

[2]

Lesson 14

1

kangaroo best soon hopping

sitting ever back fix

think runner bag pocket

pop were still cold

must kept more well

2

A	B
make	time
maker	timer
making	timing

3

rate rater rating

4

ice out very show

helped one there my

now hopped day are

stopped before where

yelled dropped began

5

(a) sitting rate pocket now runner

(b) think maker well pop ever

(c) making must stopped still kept

(d) timing helped bag soon hopping

(e) best runner fix were time

6 Kit, the Kangaroo

Kit was a kangaroo. Kangaroos hop. Kit hopped as well as the best kangaroos. But one day, she stopped hopping. She said, "I can not hop." She was very sad.

A little rat was sitting next to Kit. He said, "I can help you hop."

Kit asked, "How can you do that?"

The rat said, "Let me show you how. I will be back soon. And when I get back, you will hop as well as you ever hopped before."

[1]

When the rat got back, he had a big bag. He said, "This will fix you up."

He had a big chunk of ice in the bag. He dropped the ice in Kit's pocket. As soon as he dropped the ice, Kit began to hop. She hopped up ten feet and yelled, "Get that ice out of my pock, pock, pocket."

But the ice did not pop out. She hopped up 16 feet, but the ice still did not pop out.

[1]

Kit said, "I am so cold that I can not stop hop, hop, hopping."

The rat said, "But you must keep on hopping or that ice will not pop out."

Kit kept on hopping. At last, she stopped. She said, "I can hop no more."

The rat said, "I can help you hop."

"No," Kit said. "You helped me hop before. Now I will help you." She helped that rat hop as well as a kangaroo.

How do you think she did that?

[1]

Lesson 15

1

ea eats smear ears hear

2

fast too store much

packs must things

gum bit still

plan more chomping

3

these here ate rate

make gave like

4

A	B
hope	rider
ride	hoping
shape	later
late	shaped

5

some don't lie work oats

slow slowly show happy

give one began happened

very Sandy manner

down better planning how you

there ice out are question

6

(a) chomping bit rate more eats

(b) smear hoping gum plan too

(c) shape must store fast here

(d) much ride still packs late

(e) things gave later these plan

7

The Rat That Had a Fast Rate

Sandy had a rat that ate fast. She said, "That rat eats too 13
much. I must make the rat slow down." 21

Sandy went to the store and got ten packs of gum. She said, 34
"I will smear the gum on the oats." Then she gave the oats to 48
the rat. "Here are some oats," she said. "You will have fun 60
eating them." 62

The rat began eating at a very fast rate. But then the rate 75
began to go down. 79

[1]

The rat chomped and chomped. The rat said, "I like oats, 90
but these oats are not fun. I am chomping as fast as I can, but 105
the oats don't go down." 110

Sandy said, "Ho, ho. There is gum on them so that you can 123
not eat at a fast rate." 129

The rat said, "Give me the oats that do not have gum on 142
them, and I will eat slowly." 148

Sandy said, "I am happy to hear that." 156

[1]

She gave the rat oats that did not have gum on them. The rat 170
did 2 things. She bit Sandy's hand. Then she ate the oats at a 184
very fast rate. 187

Sandy said, "You little rat. You told me a lie." 197

The rat said, "Yes, but did you see how fast I did it?" 210

Sandy said, "I will still get you to eat slowly. You will see. I 224
have one more plan for you." 230

[1]

Lesson 16

1

ea mean eat beans meat

2

fast box plan too after help

bit began will left flash next

3

ate made nose here those these rope

4

into even didn't seven come

hopped oats don't rooms

lie chomped slow slowly

show are dropping slammed

some work days who

5

Sandy's Plan for the Rat's Fast Rate

Sandy's rat ate at a fast rate. The rat ran at a fast rate. And it 16
even hopped at a fast rate. Sandy had a plan to make the rat's 30
rate go down. 33

Sandy got a rat that did not eat at a fast rate and did not run 49
fast. This rat was fat. It sat and sat. When this rat ate, it 63
chomped slowly. Sandy said, "I will take this slow rat and show 75
my fast rat how to be slow." Sandy dropped the fat rat into the 89
box with the fast rat. 94

[1]

Lesson 16

The fast rat said, "This fat rat needs help. It is too fat. I will 109
show it how to go fast." 115

Sandy's rat bit the fat rat on the nose. "Stop that," he said. 128

Sandy's rat said, "Make me stop." 134

The fat rat began to run after Sandy's rat. These rats ran and 147
ran and ran. Then the fat rat said, "I must rest. I need to eat 162
some oats." 164

Sandy's rat said, "If you don't eat fast, I will eat these oats 177
and then no oats will be left for you." 186

"No," the fat rat said. "I can eat as fast as the next rat." And 201
it did. 203

[1]

The fat rat was in the box with the fast rat for seven days. At 218
the end of the seven days, the fat rat was not fat. It was fast. 233
When Sandy dropped oats into the box, the rats ate the oats in 246
a flash. Then the rats began to run in the box. They ran so fast 261
that Sandy said, "I cannot see those rats. I hope they slow 273
down." 274

Sandy's rat said, "This fat rat didn't make me go slow. I 286
made his rate go up. Ho, ho." 293

[1]

Lesson 17

1

oa boat float coat soap

2

went job fix smell beans

rest hammer hold began

bath for seating better

beef left cannot room meat

3

came gave make plates here

4

your other answer care

boards broken table seven

fixed some come do handed

woman grabbed asked even

into didn't slow show

work other your who

5

Champ at the Camp

A man named Champ went down a road. He came to a 12
camp. He stopped and said, "I hate to work, but I need to eat. 26
So I will see if I can get a job at this camp." So Champ went to 43
the woman who ran the camp. Champ said, "Can I work at this 56
camp? I can do lots of jobs here." 64

The camp woman said, "Are you a tramp?" 72

Champ said, "No, I am a champ at camp work." 82

"Can you fix lamps?" 86

"Yes," Champ said. 89
"Can you make boat ramps?" 94
"Yes," said Champ. "I am the champ at ramps." 103
[1]

The camp woman said, "Then I will let you work at this 115
camp." The camp woman gave Champ a hammer. She said, 125
"Take this hammer and make a ramp for these boats." 135
Champ got boards and began to hammer. When the sun went 146
down, he had made the boat ramp. He said, "Now I have to eat." 160
But the woman from the camp did not let Champ rest. She 172
handed Champ a broken lamp. Then she said, "Take these 182
clamps and fix this lamp." 187
So Champ got a clamp to hold the lamp. He fixed the lamp. 200
[1]

The camp woman said, "Now you must take a bath. I can 212
tell from your smell that you are not a champ at baths." 224
Champ said, "No, baths are not for me." 232
"You will take a bath or you will not eat," the camp woman 245
told Champ. 247
Champ ran to the eating table and grabbed ham and beef. 258
Champ said, "I don't care if I smell. I can work better than 271
the others in this camp." 276
A woman asked, "Do you think that you can work better 287
than the rest of us?" 292
Champ did not answer. He ate six plates of ham and seven 304
plates of beef. 307
Then he said, "Now I can sleep." And he went to sleep at the 321
table. The others left. They said, "We cannot stand the smell in 333
here." 334
[2]

Lesson 18

1

oa roads soaped board float

2

slept felt each ruts held

path between let's cannot

cheered hammered beat meat

holding bath short soon

3

name frame woke mile lake

nose came gave pole

4

women because their

pound himself woman

rested seven seventy

day way shows who

your others answer

broken even very some

come don't table worker

5

Champ Has a Meet with Sam

Champ slept at the table. The next day he woke up and felt 13
rested. He went to the woman who ran the camp. The woman 25
held her nose as she said, "You smell, Champ. Will you take a 38
bath?" 39

"No," Champ said. 42

Just then, a big man named Sam came up. He held his nose 55
and said, "Champ, you <u>are</u> not the champ worker at this camp. 67
I am." 69

A woman said, "Let's have a meet between Champ and 79
Sam." 80

So the men and women set things up for the big meet. They 93
gave a tamping pole to each man. They said, "We will see how 106
well Champ can tamp." 110

[1]

They went to the hill. The camp woman said, "Take these 121
tamping poles and see how fast you can pound the ruts from 133
this path." 135

Sam and Champ began tamping. They tamped the path for 145
three miles. Sam was a very fast tamper. But Champ tamped 156
faster. The men and women did not cheer for Champ. They 167
said, "Champ can tamp fast, but Sam can make ramps faster 178
than Champ can." 181

So Champ and Sam went to the lake. The camp woman said, 193
"Each man will clamp seventy boards and hammer the boards 203
on a frame. The man with the faster rate will win this meet." 216

[1]

Sam grabbed a clamp and began clamping boards. But 225
Champ clamped faster than Sam. And Champ hammered 233
faster than Sam. 236

Sam said, "I cannot work as fast as Champ because I have to 249
keep holding my nose when I work. I can beat him in a bath 263
meet." 264

Champ said, "No way." 268
The men and women cheered. They said, "Let's have a bath 279
meet." 280
The camp woman handed soap to each man. The men ran to 292
the lake with their soap. Each man soaped himself. 301
Champ beat Sam. Champ said, "That shows that I am the 312
champ of the camp. I can clamp. I can tamp. I can even take a 327
bath faster than you." 331

[2]

Lesson 19

1

seen told goat smells

each well faster just

going shore standing

bent chop kept beat

boater bath cleaning soap

beans best reached cheered

2

gave lake nose broke ate

3

brother another paddle

other woman women clapped

workers your have

who because himself their

how down day say very

slow where began table

4

Champ's Brother Has a Boat Meet

One day a man came to the camp. This man was big and fat. 14
He smelled as bad as a goat. He went up to the camp woman 28
and said, "My name is Bob. I do not like to work, but I have to 44
eat. And I am the best worker you have seen." 54

Champ, who was champ of the camp, went up to the camp 66
woman and said, "That is Big Bob, my brother." 75

[1]

Big Bob said, "No. You can't be my brother. My brother is fat, and he smells. But you are not fat, and you do not smell."

Champ said, "But I am your brother."

The camp woman said, "We do not need more workers in this camp."

Champ said, "But you need boaters. And Big Bob is the best there is."

The camp woman held her nose. She said, "We will see how well Big Bob can do in a boat meet with Sam."

Each man got in a boat. But Big Bob had an old boat that was very slow.

[1]

The camp woman said, "When I clap, begin paddling. Paddle as fast as you can to the other shore of the lake."

The camp woman clapped, and the men began to paddle. Soon Big Bob's boat was next to Sam's boat. Just then, Bob's paddle broke, and Bob's boat began to slow down. Sam's boat kept on going. The camp woman was standing on the shore. She said, "Big Bob cannot beat Sam now."

Bob bent down and began to paddle with his hands. His hands went chop, chop, chop into the lake. And his old boat began to go faster and faster.

[1]

Before Sam reached the other shore, Big Bob went past him. Men and women cheered. Even the camp woman said, "Bob is the best paddler I have seen."

Then the others said, "Let's get brother Bob to take a bath." They held their noses and ran to Big Bob. They went in the lake with him and began cleaning him with soap. When Big Bob left the lake, he did not smell.

Lesson 19

The men and women said, "Now, let's go to the eating table." 362
So Champ and his brother and the other workers went to the 374
eating table, where they ate and ate meat and beans. 384

[1]

Lesson 20

1

shed lock fix horn

pen his pick tock

fell bang reached

keep bop seen

ever broom hear

2

A	B
pole	later
broke	likes
late	poles
note	liking
came	broken
like	notes

3

door someone handle from

even now because

brother very every show

grabbed who paddle locked

clocked these those hammers

tamping bother another

4

The Clock Maker at the Camp

Champ and his brother Big Bob went to the shed. Champ 11
grabbed the handle of the door. He said, "This door has a lock 24
on it. How will we get in this shed? The hammers and the 37
tamping poles are in here. We need hammers and tampers if we 49
are to work." 52

Big Bob said, "Brother, don't bother with that lock. I will 63
kick the door in." 67

"No," Champ said. "Let's go to the camp woman and see if 79
she can get in this shed." 85

So they went to the camp woman. She said, "I will get a man 99
to fix that lock." 103

[1]

Later, an old man came to the camp. He had a big bag and a 118
big horn that he held to his ear. 126

He said, "I am here to fix a clock." 135

The men said, "We do not need someone to fix a clock. We 148
need someone to fix a lock. We cannot get in the shed because 161
the door is locked." 165

The old man said, "You say the door is clocked?" 175

Big Bob said, "Make a note for the old man. Even with his 188
ear horn, he cannot hear." 193

So Champ got a pen and made a note. The note said, "We 206
need to get in that shed, but the shed is locked." 217

The old man said, "I cannot help you. I work on clocks, not 230
locks." 231

[2]

So Big Bob got a pick and began to pick the lock. The lock 245
began to go, "Tick, tick, tock, tock." 252

Champ said, "This lock is ticking like a clock." 261

The old man grabbed a hammer from his bag and hit the 273
lock with his hammer. The lock fell from the door. The lock 285
went, "Bing, bang, bop." 289

The men went into the shed and got their tamping poles and 301
their hammers. Then they went to work. The old man picked 312
up the broken lock and said, "I will keep this clock. It is the 326
best clock I have seen." 331

[1]

Lesson 21

1

con road lid mop

near shore faster loading

slop must eating prop

glad each left moon

clean crack tore bits

begin mess sold

2

came take like slope

these those hate

3

dropped fatter grabbed mopped

slopping conned mopping

4

dollars seventeen how because

other handle door from

someone yelled ever every

give handed works what

workers brother another

5 Champ Meets the Con Man

A con man came to the camp. That con man came up the camp road with a box. The camp woman met him.

The con man dropped his box and held the lid up. He grabbed a mop from the box. He said, "The workers will like this mop. It is fatter than other mops. So a worker can mop faster with this mop."

The camp woman said, "I will get someone to take that mop and see how well it works." So the camp woman yelled for Champ.

[1]

Champ was on a slope near a shore of the lake. Was he making a ramp? No, he was raking slop near the pond. He was a fast slop raker. He went to the con man and the camp woman. The camp woman handed the mop to Champ.

"Here," she said. "See if this fatter mop mops faster than other mops."

Champ said, "I hate to stop slopping to do some mopping."

The camp woman said, "When I say that you must mop, you must mop. So take this fat mop and begin mopping."

[1]

But Champ did not begin mopping. He went to the eating table and said, "I will prop this mop near the door, and I will sit. Then I will go back and tell the others that I mopped." So that is what Champ did.

After he sat, he went back to the camp woman and the con man. He said, "Yes, this fat mop is the best mop I have ever seen."

The camp woman told the con man, "We will take seventeen 266
of those fatter mops." 270
The con man was glad to sell the mops. He handed 281
seventeen mops to the camp woman and told the camp woman, 292
"Give me 500 dollars." 296

[1]

When that con man left, the camp woman yelled for her 307
workers. She handed each woman and man a mop. Then she 318
said, "Take these mops and clean every crack in this camp." 329
Those workers began to mop. But the mops did not work. 340
When they got wet, they tore into little bits. A woman said, 352
"These mops make a mess." 357
That con man had sold the camp woman bad mops. He had 369
conned her. He got 500 dollars from the camp woman, and she 381
had seventeen mop handles and a big mess. 389

[1]

Lesson 22

1

dress near road lead

shed stream chips shack

order bench gloom coat

basket deal thank that's

free grass lunch

2

late slope these those five

3

cook folks throw I've can't

one of dollars seventeen who

day play didn't worked packer

what matter where dressed

lifted show begin because between

4

Cathy and a Band at the Bend

Cathy worked in a dress shop. One day she said, "I need a 13
rest." So she went to her pal, Pam. She said, "Pam, let us go to 28
hear a band play. A band is near the bend in the road. They 42
play well." 44

Then Cathy and Pam went to hear the band. When they got 56
near the bend in the road, Pam said, "I need to eat. Let me 70
lead you to a little shed. It is near the stream. They sell fish and 85
chips in that shed." 89

[1]

So Pam led Cathy to the fish shed near the stream. The 101
shack was packed with folks. The folks were yelling, "I was 112
next. Give me my order of fish and chips." 121

Pam said, "This is a mess." 127

Cathy and Pam left the fish shed and sat on a bench. A man 141
came up to them. He had a net, and he was dressed in a big 156
coat. He set the net in the sand, and then he sat down on the 171
bench. He asked Cathy, "What is the matter?" 179

Cathy said, "The shed is packed. We will be late to hear the 192
band." 193

[1]

The man said, "I am a fish packer. If you need fish, let me 207
help you." 209

The man went to his boat in the stream. Then he came back 222
with a basket. Cathy said, "Let me pay you for those fish." 234

"Give me five dollars," the man said. 241

"That is a deal," Cathy said. "Thank you." 249

She said to Pam, "I've got lots of fish." 258

Pam said, "But those fish are not cooked." 266

"I didn't think of that," Cathy said. 273

Then Cathy grabbed the basket of fish and ran into the fish 285
shed. 286

[1]

"What are you going to do?" Pam asked. 294

Cathy said to the man in the fish shed, "Cook these fish, and 307
you can keep five of them." 313

"That's a deal," the man said. 319

After the man fixed the fish, Pam said, "Can you throw in 331
some free chips?" The man did that. 338

Then Cathy and Pam left the shed near the stream. When 350
they got to the band at the bend in the road, they set their 364
basket of fish in the grass. Then they sat on a bench to hear the 379
band and eat their lunch. 384

[1]

Lesson 23

1

cold store that read back

soon job beans helped

ham better things much

2

name like came note bone home

3

Gretta Chee let's day pay played

stay someone saying door bigger said

I've cook other some don't can't

folks didn't another their became one

4

Chee, the Dog

Gretta got a little dog. She named the dog Chee. Chee got 12
bigger and bigger each day. 17

On a very cold day, Gretta said, "Chee, I must go to the 30
store. You stay home. I will be back." 38

Chee said, "Store, lots, of, for, no." 45

Then Gretta said, "Did I hear that dog say things?" 55

Chee said, "Say things can I do." 62

Gretta said, "Dogs don't say things. So I must not hear 73
well." 74

But Chee did say things. Gretta left the dog at home. When 86
Gretta came back, Chee was sitting near the door. 95

[1]

Gretta said, "That dog is bigger than she was." 104
Then the dog said, "Read, read for me of left." 114
Gretta said, "Is that dog saying that she can read?" Gretta 125
got a pad and made a note for the dog. The note said, "Dear 139
Chee, if you can read this note, I will hand you a bag of bones." 154
Gretta said, "Let's see if you can read." 162
Chee said, "Dear Chee, if you can read this note, I will ham 175
you a bag for beans." 180

[1]

Gretta said, "She can read, but she can't read well. Ho, ho." 192
Chee became very mad. She said, "For note don't read ho ho." 204
Gretta said, "Chee gets mad when I say ho, ho." 214
Chee said, "Yes, no go ho ho." 221
Then Gretta felt sad. She said, "I didn't mean to make you 233
mad. I don't like you to be sad. I will help you say things well." 248
Then Chee said, "Yes, well, of say for things." 257
So every day, Gretta helped Chee say things. She helped 267
Chee read, too. 270

[1]

Chee got better and better at saying things. And she got 281
better at reading. And she got bigger and bigger. When she was 293
one year old, she was bigger than Gretta. 301
On a hot day, Gretta left Chee at home, but when she got 314
back, Chee met her at the door. "Did you have fun at your 327
job?" Chee asked. 330

"Yes, I did," Gretta said. 336

"I don't have much fun at home," Chee said. "I think I will 349
get a job. I don't like to stay at home." 359

"Dogs can't have jobs," Gretta said. 365

Chee said, "You have a job. So I will get a job, too." 378

[1]

Lesson 24

1

clock hear locked near

conning pack road met

corn shed sled told

sack deal horn room

2

A	B
make	trades
like	maker
trade	saving
save	liked
	traded

3

ready folks from show grow

grower dressed don't yelled

grabbed dropped handed I've

some day cook stamped

4

shade here made like trade

Lesson 24

5 The Old Clock Maker and the Con Man

The old clock maker did not hear well. He left the camp with the lock. He had this lock in his pack. He went down a road from the camp. Then he met a corn grower.

But the corn grower was not a corn grower. He was the con man dressed up like a corn grower. That con man liked conning folks.

The con man said, "Let's go sit in the shade near my shed."

"Yes," the clock maker said, "I will trade for a bed."

"No, not a bed," the con man said. "Shed. We will sit near my shed."

The clock maker said, "Yes, I like a sled, but I don't see a sled."

[1]

The con man was mad at the clock maker. He yelled, "WE WILL SIT IN THE SHADE."

"Yes," the clock maker said. "I am ready to trade."

The con man led the clock maker to the shade. He held the clock maker's horn to the clock maker's ear. Then he asked, "Will you trade your pack for some corn?"

"No," the clock maker said, "I need this horn. So I will not trade this horn. But I will trade my pack for corn."

The con man got a sack of corn. He set the sack near the shed.

Then the con man went into that shed and got a very big horn. He said, "Hold this horn to your ear, and you will hear me better."

[2]

The clock maker said, "Yes, that deal seems better. I will 253
trade my little horn for this big horn." 261

The clock maker grabbed the big horn and dropped it into 272
his pack. He handed his little horn to the con man. "Here," he 285
said. "Now this is your horn. We have traded horns." 295

"No, no," the con man yelled. 301

The clock maker said, "Yes, I have made my trade for the 313
day. Now I must go." So he did. 321

The con man was very mad. He stamped up and down. Then 333
he asked, "How did that man con me out of my horn? He has 347
the big horn, and I just have a little horn and some corn." 360

[1]

Lesson 25

1

tears fun cheeks brick plant

molds speak load leave still hearing

2

felt self left get went help

3

bake here fire home

4

boss herself station

something question can't

saying from fireman didn't

patted over himself began

ready Chee Gretta upset

5

Chee Goes for a Job

Chee felt sad. So she left her home to get a job. 12
Chee went to a fire station. She went up to the man who ran 26
the station and said, "I need a job. Can you help me?" 38
The man said, "Is my hearing going bad, or did that dog say 51
something to me?" 54
The dog said, "I did say something. Do you have a job for 67
me?" 68
The man said, "Ho, ho. That dog is saying things, but dogs 80
can't speak." 82

[1]

Chee got so mad that she began to say odd things. "Fire 94
station for of to go," she said. 101

The man said, "Ho, ho. This dog is fun. I will keep this dog 115
with me. I like to hear the odd things that dog can say." 128

Chee was so mad at the fireman she said, "From of for, 140
fireman." 141

The fireman fell down and went, "Ho, ho, ho." He had tears 153
on his cheeks. His ears got red. Then he patted Chee and said, 166
"I didn't mean to make you mad. But you do say odd things." 179

[1]

Then the dog said to herself, "I will not work here. I can't 192
stand to hear that fireman go 'Ho, ho.' " 200

So Chee left the station. She went down the road to a brick 213
plant. The man in the brick plant said, "Well, well, I see a dog 227
in this plant." 230

"Yes," Chee said. Then she asked the man, "Can I have a job 243
here?" 244

The man said, "What have we here? A dog that can say 256
things." Then he asked, "Can you help bake bricks?" 265

"I think so," Chee said. 270

[1]

The man asked, "Can you fill brick molds?" 278

"Yes," Chee said. 281

Then the man said, "But you are a dog. I do not think that I 296
can hire you." The man began to think. At last he said, "I will 310
get my boss. He will tell me what to do." 320

The man left and came back with his boss. The boss said to 333
Chee, "I will hire you if you can lift that load of bricks." 346

But she did not lift the bricks. She got upset and said, "Much 359
bricks lift, no." She showed her teeth. 366

The boss said, "Leave this plant." 372

So Chee left. She still did not have a job. 382

[1]

1

ranch faster chopped

goats checked horses

bent slap leave heels

loafers swam swim jab

2

rode named rider safe

makes side tame time

3

Emma anyone nobody good

because let's boss didn't

ready their Flop woman

women milked herself station

question biggest stayed Branch

4

The Rancher

There was a big ranch in the West. The rancher who ran this 13
ranch was named Emma Branch. She rode a horse well. She 24
chopped fast, and she swam faster. The men and women who 35
worked for Emma Branch liked her. They said, "She is the best 47
in the West." On her ranch she had sheep, and she had cows. 60
There were goats and horses. There was a lot of grass. 71

The rancher had a lot of women and men working for her. 83
They worked with the sheep and the goats, and they milked the 95

cows. Each worker had a horse. But the rancher's horse was the 107
biggest and the best. It was a big, black horse named Flop. 119
[1]

Flop got its name because it reared up. When Flop reared 130
up, any rider on it fell down and went "flop" in the grass. But 144
Flop did not rear up when the rancher rode it. Emma Branch 156
bent near Flop's ear and said, "Let's go, Flop." And they went. 168
She did not have to slap the horse. She didn't have to jab her 182
heels and yell at Flop. She just said, "Let's go," and they went 195
like a shot. 198

Every day, she checked up on the workers to see what they 210
were doing. She checked to see that they were working well and 222
that they were not loafing. 227
[1]

If a worker was loafing, Emma told the worker, "I will say 239
this for the last time: 'Do not loaf on this ranch any more.' " If 253
a worker was loafing the next time she checked, she said, "Go 265
from my ranch. We do not need loafers here." 274

The women and men who worked on the ranch said, "When 285
you hear Flop running, you had better be working. If you are 297
not working, you had better get ready to leave this ranch." 308

But the workers that stayed at the ranch liked to work for 320
Emma Branch. They said, "We like to have Emma on our side. 332
We can see how mean Flop is, and he is very tame when Emma 346
rides him. So it's good to have Emma on your side." 357
[2]

Lesson 27

1

plant tears stacks kept sore

Chee cheeks easy just slab

2

A	B	C
slow	slowest	slowly
near	nearly	nearest
safe	safest	safely
fast	faster	fastest

3

slate came pile rate side

4

money you'll look good

things sense clapped may

saying showed hands way

think picked that's odd

worked cannot began ever

because added stackers

never anyone nobody

5

Chee Stacks Slate

Chee went to get a job, but no plant had jobs for dogs that 14
say things. At last, Chee went to a slate plant. Chee said, "I 27
hope that I can get a job here." Chee went into the plant. Chee 41
went past stacks of slate. She came to the woman who ran the 54
plant. Chee asked, "Do you have a job I can do in this plant?" 68

The woman looked at Chee. Then the woman said, "Ho, ho, 79
ho. I cannot help going 'Ho, ho, ho.' " 87

[1]

Chee got so mad that she began to say odd things. "Stop 99
slate for from me, of go so no to do, ho ho." 111

The woman fell down and kept going "Ho, ho, ho." 121

Chee felt so mad that she did not stop saying odd things. 133

The woman got sore from going "Ho, ho." She had lots of 145
tears on her cheeks. Then she stopped ho-hoing and said, "I 156
have seen lots of things, but I have never seen a dog that said 170
odd things." 172

[1]

Chee was not so mad now. So Chee began to say things that 185
made sense. Chee said, "I told you not to go 'Ho, ho.' I told you 200
that I need a job." 205

The woman got up and clapped her hands. She said, "Let me 217
see. I think I may have a job for you." The woman's cheeks still 231
had tears on them. She asked, "Can you stack slate?" 241

Chee said, "I think so." 246

The woman showed Chee how to stack slate. 254

[1]

The woman said, “Stacking is easy. You just pick up a slab 267
of slate and set it on top of your pile.” Chee picked up a slab 282
and set it on the pile. 288

“That’s the way to do it,” the woman said. Then she added, 300
“See how fast you can stack. The faster you stack, the more 312
money you’ll make.” 315

So Chee began her job as a slate stacker. Each day, her rate 328
went up. She worked at the plant for nearly a year. At the end 342
of the year, she was one of the fastest stackers in the plant. 351

[1]

Lesson 28

1

shearing helper than locks

pants sheets planned holding

steal still chest every

2

hope rate shaved nose fake those

3

A	B	C
shape	shaping	shapely
like	likely	liked
cold	coldest	colder
short	shortly	shortest

4

wool look good even

stay show felt ready

someone where there

money before grabbed

5 The Con Man and the Sheep Rancher

Emma Branch had a lot of big sheep on her ranch. One day 13
she said, "My sheep need shearing. I will send for a sheep 25
shearer." 26

So she told one of her helpers to go to town and get someone 40
who can shear sheep. The helper went down the road to town. 52
But he did not get there. He met the con man on the road. The 67
con man said, "Where are you going?" 74

The helper said, "The rancher needs her sheep sheared." 83

The con man said, "I am the best at shearing sheep. I have 96
shears in my pack." 100

So Emma's helper led the con man back to the ranch. When 112
they got there, Emma yelled from the door, "I hope that man 124
can shear fast." 127

[1]

The con man said, "I can shave sheep. I can shape. And I 140
can shear." 142

"But how is your rate at shearing?" the rancher asked. 152

"I can go so fast that I can shave a sheep before it sees the 167
shears. You can shop and shop, but you cannot get someone 178
who can shape or shave faster than me." 186

So the con man got the job. He told the rancher to get him 200
ten sacks for holding the wool. 206

The con man had a plan. He did not plan to shear sheep. He 220
planned to steal sheep. He planned to pack sheep into sacks. 231
Then he planned to take those sacks and run from the ranch. 243

[1]

But his plan did not work very well. The rancher did not 255
leave him. She said, "I will stay and see how fast you shear." 268
The con man had never sheared sheep before. He got the 279
shears from his pack and grabbed a sheep. The sheep ran from 291
the con man. The rancher said, "Ho, ho. You can't even hold a 304
sheep. Let me show you how." The rancher grabbed a sheep 315
and sat on its nose. Then she said, "Now I've got this sheep. 328
You shave it." 331
The con man began to shave that sheep, but the sheep did 343
not stay still. 346

[1]

The con man shaved the rancher's leg. Then the con man 357
shaved the hay near the sheep. Then the con man shaved his 369
hand. 370
"Ho, ho," the rancher said. "You are a fake. You cannot 381
shave sheep. You have never held shears before. Let me show 392
you how to do that job." 398
She grabbed the con man and held him down. She sat on his 411
back and began to shave him. She shaved his locks. She shaved 423
his coat. She shaved his pants. She shaved his legs. She even 435
shaved his chest. When he was shaved, she said, "Now you see 447
how to shave. Pack up your shears and leave this ranch." 458
When the con man left the ranch, he felt very cold. 469

[2]

Lesson 29

1

nearly slop more year

bum rest bath morning

stack flash weeks deal

2

lake raked shade time

rider take shaved fake

3

person believe any beans

town stay show seven

happened hammers boards

look women wool can't

where conning workers

4

The Rancher and Champ

Champ had worked at the camp for nearly a year. He had 12
tamped and made ramps. He had fixed lamps and raked slop 23
near the lake. But now he said, "I think I will leave this camp. I 38
am a champ, and champs don't stay in the same camp for more 51
than a year." 54

So Champ got his pack and went to the camp woman. He 66
told her, "I must go now. The work here is getting old, and I 80
need a rest. I will go sit in the shade and eat beans and rest. It 96
is time to go where I do not have to take a bath." 109

[1]

So Champ left and went down the camp road. When he got to a town, he said, "I see a person on a big black horse. I will ask that rider where I can go to rest in the shade." Champ went up to the person on the black horse and said, "Tell me, where can I go to rest in the shade?"

The person on the horse was Emma Branch. She was the rancher that shaved the con man. She said, "I help men and women who work well."

"I work well," Champ said. "But I am sick of working. I need a rest."

[1]

Then the rancher said to Champ, "I can tell that you do not like to work. Are you a tramp?"

That made Champ mad. He said, "I am a champ, not a tramp. I like to work. And I can work better than any of the workers on your ranch. I work faster than any ranch hand you have ever seen."

"Ho, ho," the rancher said. "The last man who said he was a fast worker did not do a thing. He was a fake. And I think you are a fake, too."

Champ got so mad that he got a hammer from his sack. He went to a stack of boards. In a flash, Champ made a little shed from those boards.

[1]

The rancher did not believe what happened. Then she said, "That was the fastest hammering I have ever seen. But how are you at shearing sheep?"

"I can shear faster than I can hammer," Champ said. 372

The rancher said, "If you show me that you can shear sheep 384
that fast, I will let you sit in the shade on my ranch for seven 399
weeks. But if you are conning me, I will hold you down and 412
shave you." 414

Champ said, "It is a deal." 420

So the rancher and Champ went to the ranch. The rancher 431
said, "When the sun comes up in the morning, we will see how 444
well you shear." 447

[2]

Lesson 30

1

near felt morning heaps

flashed sweeping reached

shears melt jerk plop worker

2

wake nose shaving five

3

minutes handed rested may

wool cannot work have any

grabbed wow out seven

slow sleeping look took

good cook very down

don't believe person yelled

4

Champ Shows the Rancher How to Shear

The sun came up in the morning. Champ was sleeping near a 12
big sheep shed. The rancher's helper came to wake him up. 23

Champ said, "Leave me be. I am sleeping." So Champ went 34
back to sleep. 37

The helper ran to Emma and said, "That Champ didn't get 48
up when I went to wake him up." 56

Emma grabbed shears and ran over to Champ. Her helper 66
ran with her. When they got to Champ, the rancher handed her 78

shears to her helper. She said to Champ, "If you don't get up, 91
my helper will give you a shearing." 98
So Champ got up and went to the sheep shed with Emma. 110
[1]

Emma said, "We have a deal. If you can shear 50 sheep as 123
fast as you hammer, you may stay and rest on my ranch." 135
Then she handed the shears to Champ. Champ felt more like 146
sleeping than shearing. He said, "I did not sleep well. When I 158
am not rested, I cannot work well. I will have to jump up and 172
down to wake up." So Champ began to jump up and down. 184
Then he said, "Now I can shear sheep." 192
"Good," Emma said. "You have 50 minutes to shear 50 202
sheep." Like a flash, Champ went for a sheep. 211
[1]

He grabbed the sheep and sat on its nose. His shears flashed 223
in the sun. And wool went plop, plop from the sheep. The 235
rancher said, "Wow! That's fast shearing. This man has made 245
heaps and heaps of wool." 250
Champ was shearing sheep faster than the helper was 259
sweeping up the wool. "Slow down," the helper yelled. "I 269
cannot sweep that fast." 273
Champ said, "Don't tell me to slow down, or I will take 285
these shears and give you a shaving." 292
In less than five minutes, those 50 sheep had been sheared. 303
Then Champ handed the shears to the rancher. "Here," he 313
said. "I have sheared these sheep." 319
The rancher dropped the shears. "They are hot," she said. 329
[1]

Champ said, “When I shear sheep, I go so fast that the 341
shears may melt.” 344

The rancher asked, “Where is my helper? I do not see him.” 356

“Is he in that heap of wool?” Champ asked. 365

“Yes, yes,” the helper said. “I am in a heap, and I cannot see 379
one thing.” 381

Champ reached into the heap and grabbed the helper’s hand. 391
He gave the hand a jerk. And out came a helper. The rancher 404
said, “Champ can shear sheep faster than you can sweep wool.” 415

So Emma kept her deal with Champ. Champ rested on her 426
ranch for seven weeks. And every day, the helper took big 437
meals to Champ. Each day, Champ just rested and ate. He did 449
no work. 451

[2]

Lesson 31

1

meals between until

horse plan win

better bets shearing

2

A	B	C
neat	neatly	neatest
broke	broken	broker
year	yearly	years
beat	beater	beaten

3

ate lake shade shaved

shame like shape

4

Shelly people stayed wool

bragged anyone town dollars

other slower have look

things handed hated rested

week don't didn't let's

Lesson 31

5 The Rancher Sets Up a Shearing Meet

Champ had stayed at the ranch for seven weeks. Every day, he 12
had big meals of beef and ham and beans and corn. Every day, 25
he sat in the shade near the lake. And every day, he got a little 40
slower. He got slower and slower with each meal that he ate. 52

The rancher did not think that Champ was slow. She had 63
seen him go so fast that the helper did not sweep the wool as 77
fast as Champ shaved sheep. 82

Emma went to town and bragged. She said, "There is a man on 95
my ranch who can shear sheep faster than anyone you have seen." 107

[1]

When Emma was in town one day, she told a lot of people, 120
"A man on my ranch can beat anyone in a shearing meet." 132

A woman named Shelly stepped up to Emma and said, "I 143
think I can beat anyone in a shearing meet." 152

"Let's have a meet," the others yelled. 159

"Yes," the rancher said. 163

So they set up a meet between Champ and Shelly. A man 175
said, "Let's make bets. I will bet on Shelly. I have seen her 188
work with shears, and I think she can beat any other worker." 200

The rancher said, "I will bet ten dollars on my champ." Then 212
she made other bets. 216

[1]

When Emma got back to the ranch, she told Champ, "Your 227
seven weeks are up. If you stay, you will have to work." 239

"That is a shame," he said. "I hate to work. So I will have to 254
leave." 255

The rancher said, "I will make a deal with you. We will have 268
a shearing meet between you and Shelly. If you win that meet, 280
you may stay here on my ranch. And you will not have to work 294
every day. I will make you do a little work now and then. But if 309
you do not win the meet, you will have to work like a horse." 323
Champ said, "Yes, I like that plan." 330

[1]

The rancher said, "We will have that meet at the end of this 343
week. So get in shape." 348
"Yes, yes," the fat champ said. 354
"I mean it," the rancher said. "You seem to be in bad shape. 367
You have rested for seven weeks. Now you don't look like you 379
can do things very fast." 384
Champ said, "Well, I am the best, and I will win that 396
shearing meet. But I will need a lot of rest until the day of the 411
meet." 412
"I hope you can shear better than you look," Emma said. 423
"Yes, yes," Champ said. And then he went back to sleep. 434

[2]

Lesson 32

1

told corn faster sheared

cheered pick beaten flash

west heap sore speed

2

shape shaved hope

pile fake shamed

3

all slower turn anyone

down town before wool into

landed rested melted others

yelled Shelly every begin

working now dropping show

4

The Shearing Meet

The rancher had told Champ to get in shape for the shearing 12
meet. But did Champ get in shape? No. He ate big meals of 25
corn and ham and beans and meat. Then he went to sleep. 37

Was Champ in shape at the end of the week? No. Champ 49
was out of shape and very slow. 56

People from town came to the ranch with Shelly. Shelly was 67
in tip-top shape. Before the meet began, she sheared a sheep to 79
show the others how fast she was. Before the wool that fell from 92
the sheep had landed, that sheep was shaved from one end to 104
the other. 106

[1]

The people cheered. "Shelly can beat anyone at shearing," 115
they yelled. 117

Champ had to work to pick up the shears. He said, "I may 130
have rested too much, but when I get going, I will speed up." 143

The rancher said, "Shelly and Champ will shear all day." 153

Champ said to his helper, "I hope you are fast at sweeping. 165
This wool will be dropping very fast." 172

The rancher said, "Go," and the shearing began. 180

[1]

Champ's shears did not go like a flash. And the wool did not 193
pile up fast. "I must go faster," he said. But he did not go faster. 208
He went slower. He ran the shears into the sheep's ear, and the 221
sheep bit him on the leg. Then the sheep got up and ran from 235
the shed. 237

The people said, "Ho, ho. Champ can't shear. But Shelly is 248
going like a shot." 252

Shelly had sheared three sheep, and she was working on the 263
next sheep. Her helper was up to his ears in wool. "I need 276
help," the helper yelled. 280

[1]

Champ's helper said, "I can help you now. Champ is so slow 292
that he will never make a pile of wool." 301

So Champ's helper began to help Shelly's helper. And 310
Champ went to get the sheep that ran from him. When he got 323
the sheep, Shelly had shaved seven more sheep. 331

Champ and Shelly sheared for the rest of the day. When the 343
sun was going down in the west, Shelly had sheared 500 sheep. 355
Champ had sheared 40 sheep. Shelly had melted three shears. 365
Champ's shears were cold. 369

[1]

Lesson

32

Shelly had made a heap of wool as big as a hill. Champ had 383
made a pile of wool as big as ten sheep. 393

Emma was yelling at Champ. “You are a fake.” 402

The rancher said to the others, “My champ did not win this 414
meet, so I will pay you for the bets that I made.” 426

When the other people left, the rancher went to Champ. She 437
said, “In the morning, you are going to begin work. And you 449
will work like a horse every day.” 456

Champ felt bad. He did not say a thing. He was sore. He was 470
shamed. He had never been beaten in a meet before. 480

[1]

Lesson 33

1

peeking picked more dug sore

hammer east beginning lend next

2

ate gate holes shape

gave shaving five

3

you're could worked egg handed

may very every even all

there another dollars people

seventy others odds one

any meal beaten broken

ready three boards planted

4

Champ Gets in Shape

Champ worked and worked at the ranch. Every day, he got 11
up when the sun was peeking over the hill in the east. Champ 24
did not eat a big meal. He went to the sheep shed and sheared 38
sheep. Then he picked corn. Then he ate a little meal. He had 51
an egg and a little bit of ham. He said, "I need more to eat." 66

"No more," the rancher said. "Back to work for you." She 77
handed Champ a hammer. "Take boards and make a gate," she 88
said. 89

[1]

After Champ had made a gate, the rancher said, "Now take 100
boards and make a pen for goats." After Champ had made a 112

pen of boards, she said, "Next, you're going to dig holes for 124
planting trees." 126

So Champ dug ten tree holes. Then he planted three trees. 137
Then he sheared more sheep. At last, the rancher said, "Now 148
you may eat a meal." 153

But it was a very little meal. Champ ate it and said, "I need 167
more to eat." 170

"No more," she said. And she gave Champ more work. 180

[1]

At the end of the day, Champ was sore. He was sore the next 194
day. 195

But at the end of the week, he began to get faster. His hammer 209
began to go like a flash. His shears began to get hot when he was 224
shaving sheep. Champ was beginning to get back in shape. 234

Champ worked for five weeks. And he got a little faster every 246
week. He had worked so fast that there was no more work at the 260
ranch. So he went to the rancher and said, "Send your helper to 273
town and tell Shelly that I am ready for another shearing meet." 285

[1]

The rancher said, "I will send my helper to town. But I will 298
not make bets on you." 303

Champ said, "I will bet on me. Lend me seventy dollars." 314

So the rancher lent seventy dollars to Champ. Then she sent 325
her helper to town. The helper told people, "Champ says he 336
can beat Shelly in a shearing meet." 343

The others said, "Ho, ho." 348

The rancher's helper told them, "But Champ will bet that he 359
can beat Shelly. He has seventy dollars, and he will bet if he 372
gets odds." 374

[1]

Shelly said, "Champ is so bad at shearing that he needs very 386
big odds. I will bet at three-to-one odds." 394

"So will I," the others said. 400

So the helper bet Champ's seventy dollars at three-to-one 409
odds. He said, "This means that Champ will get 210 dollars if 421
he beats Shelly in a meet." 427

The others said, "But we don't think there is any way he can 440
beat Shelly." 442

The helper went back to the ranch and told Champ that he 454
had made bets at three-to-one odds. 460

"I like those odds," Champ said. "I will win this next meet." 472
[1]

Lesson 34

1

ai

A	B
wait	waited
paint	pain
sail	grain
main	fail

2

beaten road cheered

real keep before

3

gates shape waved here's

saving shaved five broken

4

planted worked faster people

yelled town didn't grabbed

seventeen all wool slow

begged planned let's you're

panting handed speed ready

5

The Meet with Shelly Is Set

Champ felt he was in shape for the shearing meet. When 11
there was no more work on Emma's ranch, Champ did some 22
work at the next ranch, so he could stay in shape. He made ten 36
gates. He planted 600 trees. He sheared 950 sheep. The helpers 47

that worked on this ranch said, "He is the fastest worker in the land."

Shelly did not get in shape. She said, "I am in shape. My hands are fast. I have never been beaten in a shearing meet."

On the day of the meet, Champ sat near the ranch gate. The people from town came up the road. They waved to Champ.

[1]

The people said, "We made bets that Shelly will beat you." Then they went to the sheep shed and waited.

When Shelly came up the road, the people cheered. "Here's Shelly," they yelled.

Just before the meet began, Emma Branch came up to Champ. She said, "If you do not beat Shelly, I will not let you stay here. You will have to get your things and leave this ranch."

Champ didn't say a thing. He just sat and waited.

"We are ready for a shearing meet," a woman yelled. "Let's go."

[1]

Champ ran fast as a shot. He grabbed his shears and said, "I will need three helpers. I will make heaps of wool so fast that 2 helpers will not keep up with me."

The others said, "Ho, ho." Seven people said, "We will help with wool if you need us." Then they said, "Ho, ho."

Shelly and Champ held their shears and waited. Then the rancher said, "Go," and they began shearing. Champ went so fast that he had sheared 2 sheep before Shelly ran her shears over one sheep. When Shelly had sheared seven sheep, Champ had sheared 46 sheep.

[1]

Champ made heaps of wool so fast that his helpers yelled, "Help!"

So the seven people who had said, "We will help," began to 328
bag heaps of wool. But Champ went so fast that they did not 341
keep up with him. They begged, "Slow down. We cannot bag 352
wool this fast." 355

"No," Champ said. "I will not slow down. I have been saving 367
my real speed for the end of this meet. And here I go." Champ 381
had shaved 4 sheep as he told them what he planned to do. Now 395
he went so fast that seven more people had to help bag wool. 408

[1]

At the end of the meet, Champ had sheared 9,000 sheep. 419
Shelly had sheared 501 sheep. Seventeen people were panting. 428
They said, "We made a bad bet. Now we have to pay 440
three-to-one odds to Champ." So they did. 447

Then Champ handed his 210 dollars to the rancher and said, 458
"Now we are even. You bet on me before and I was beaten. So 472
take this 210 dollars." 476

"No," Emma said. "Pay me the seventy dollars I lent you. 487
That will make us even." Then the rancher said, "You see, I 499
made a bet on you, too. You worked so fast this week that I bet 514
100 dollars at five-to-one odds." 519

Champ said, "So now you have five hundred dollars." 528

[1]

Lesson 35

1

ai

A	B
rain	fail
grain	sailed
waited	main

2

stacker nearly luck sleeves shabby

coats room runs seated desk

3

quit yellow button else

Rop box people showed

slowly who another slam

all stepped sloppy slid

any ready one sobbed

something seventy stamped

person grabbed slapped

4

Chee Meets Rop

Chee worked as a slate stacker for nearly a year. By then, her 13
rate of stacking was very good. But she was getting a little sick 26
of her job. "Stack, stack, stack," she said. "It's time to do 38
something else." So she went to the woman who ran the slate 50
plant and said, "I think I have to quit and get another job." 63

The woman said, "You have been a good worker. Good luck." 74

Lesson 35

Chee left the plant and went looking for work. She came to a 87
sleeve plant. They made sleeves for coats in this plant. 97

[1]

Chee went into the plant and said to the people working in a 110
big room, "Where is the person who runs this plant?" 120

They went, "Ho, ho. We do not work for a person." 131

Chee told them, "You must work for someone. Show me who." 142

A man stepped up to Chee. The man said, "Step into that 154
room and you will see who runs this plant. His name is Rop." 167

So Chee stepped into the room. Then she stopped. There was 178
no man seated at the desk. There was a yellow dog at the desk. 192

[1]

The yellow dog slapped a stamp on a letter. Then he pressed 204
a button. A man came into the room. The yellow dog said, "I 217
have stamped this letter. Get it into the mail box now." 228

The man grabbed the letter and ran from the room. "Don't 239
slam the door," the yellow dog yelled. 246

The man did not slam the door. When the man had left the 259
room, the yellow dog slowly got up from the desk. He said to 272
Chee, "Leave this room. Pets cannot stay here. I told the 283
people who work for me they cannot have pets here. So go 295
home, you shabby dog." 299

[1]

"Shabby dog?" Chee said. "I am not a shabby dog, you sloppy 311
yellow dog. I am not a pet. I can do more things than you can." 326

The yellow dog showed his teeth. Then he said, "I run this 338
plant. You are just a dog. Seventy people work for me. No one 351
works for you. I make a lot of dollars each week. I'll bet that 365
you don't have one dollar. And you don't say things very well." 377

Chee showed her teeth. She was so mad that she began to say 390
odd things. 392

[1]

Chee said, "Slob, slab, you speak well, for more of people 403
beat I bet, you yellow shabby." 409
The yellow dog was ho-hoing like mad. He fell down and 420
sobbed, "Ho, ho." Tears slid from his nose. His nose got red. 432
Chee said, "Stop, you slob ho-hoing, I let for slapping of 443
your shabby yellow, you bum." 448
Then Rop stopped ho-hoing. He said, "If you think you are 459
better than me, we will have a meet. I will show you that I can 474
beat you in any meet you name." 481
Chee said, "With or of OK." 487

[1]

Lesson 36

1

sleeving fresh store slabs score

checkers slap chomp gromp

2

named scale same sale jokes

3

fantastic I'll yellow doing between

yelled going ready next other one

questions played quit sense else

slop button silly stammer yet

4

Rop and Chee Have a Meet

Chee had met a yellow dog in a sleeve plant. The yellow dog 13
was named Rop, and he ran the plant. He said that he was 26
better than Chee at doing things. Chee got mad. So a meet was 39
set between Rop and Chee. Rop said, "We will see if you can 52
beat me in this meet." 57

Rop yelled to the workers in the sleeve plant. "Stop sleeving 68
and get in here fast," he said. The workers ran into the room. 81
Rop said, "Chee and I are going to have a meet. We will begin 95
by seeing how fast we can eat." 102

[1]

Rop told a worker, "Get me 2 slabs of fresh meat. Drop the 115
slabs on the scale and see that they are the same." 126

A woman ran from the plant. She went to the store. She 138
grabbed 2 slabs of meat that were on sale. She got back to the 152

plant and dropped them on the scale. Each slab was the same.

Rop handed a slab to Chee. “Here’s your slab. See if you can keep up with me.” Then he said, “When you hear me say, ‘Go,’ get your teeth into that meat. Get set . . .”

[1]

Chee was ready to eat. She was not going to let that yellow dog beat her at eating meat.

“Go,” Rop said. And Chee went. Chomp, chomp, gromp, clop.

But Chee did not beat Rop, and Rop did not beat Chee. Their score was the same. Rop was mad. He said, “I did not beat her at eating, but I will get the best score in the next thing we do. We will tell jokes. The dog who tells the best jokes will get the best score.”

A woman said, “How can we tell if one joke is better than the other joke?”

[1]

Rop said, “It’s easy to tell which joke is better. If the workers go ‘ho, ho’ more for one joke, that joke is the better joke.”

Then Rop told his joke. This was his joke: “A woman went to see her pal. Her pal was playing checkers with a dog. The woman had never seen a dog that played checkers. So the woman said to her pal, ‘That dog is fantastic.’

“Her pal said, ‘This dog is not so hot. I beat her 2 of every three games.’ ”

The workers ho-hoed and ho-hoed.

Rop said, “Let’s see you beat that joke, you silly lap dog.”

[1]

Rop made Chee so mad that she began to stammer and say odd things.

She said, "I'll lap your slap over never checker playing with a 432
slop Rop named yellow teeth." 437

The workers ho-hoed and ho-hoed. When they stopped going 446
"ho, ho," a woman said to Rop, "We cannot tell if that dog's 459
joke was better than your joke. We think the score is the same." 472

Rop yelled, "I will get that silly lap dog yet. Let's go into the 486
sleeve-making room for the next meet that we will have." 496

Chee said, "Fantastic of checkers, with sleeves. OK." 504

[2]

Lesson 37

1

room score coats needle

champ form cutter which

tricking really holler hep

2

A	B
her	herself
him	himself
your	yourself
can	cannot
any	anybody

3

close to shame poke making

4

know first another where others

wool ready slapped sleeves

can't else ended from

lap I'll fantastic because

5

Sleeve Slapping

Chee and Rop went into the sleeve-making room of the 10
plant. There Rop said, "I will get the best score for this meet. 23
We will see how fast that lap dog can slap sleeves on coats. The 37
dog that slaps sleeves fastest will get the best score." 47

Rop handed Chee a needle. Rop said, "Take this needle and 58
get set to go. And don't stab yourself. Ho, ho." 68

Chee was mad. She held the needle and waited for Rop to 80
say, "Go." 82

Rop said, "Get set . . . go." 87

Chee went very fast, but she stabbed herself with the needle. 98

"Ow," she said. 101

[1]

"Ho, ho," Rop said, "That lap dog just stabbed herself. Ho, 112
ho, ho, hee, hee." As Rop was ho-heeing, he did not see where 125
his needle was going, and he stabbed himself. "Ow," he said. 136

"Ho, hee, hep, hep, hep," Chee said. 143

Rop yelled, "Stop. This meet is over. I have slapped seven 154
sleeves on coats. So I am the champ, and I get the best score. 168
Let's hear it for me." 173

"Stop," Chee said. "I have slapped seven sleeves on coats, 183
too. So my score is the same as yours." 192

Chee was sore where the needle went into her, but she was 204
glad that Rop had stabbed himself, too. Rop said, "Let's go to 216
the room where we form sleeves." 222

[1]

Chee, Rop, and the others went to the sleeve-forming room. 232
Rop handed Chee shears. Then he handed her a form for 243

making sleeves. He said, "Slap this form on the wool. Then 254
take your shears and cut close to the form. That's how you cut 267
sleeves from wool. Get ready . . . get set . . . go." 275

Chee slapped the form on the wool and began cutting with 286
the shears. She cut very fast. Rop cut fast, too. Rop said, 298
"Don't cut yourself, slow poke." 303

But Chee did stab herself with the shears. "Ow," she said. 314

Rop said, "Ho, ho, hee, hep, hep. Ow." 322

[1]

As Rop ho-hepped, he stabbed himself with the shears. 331

Then Rop said, "Stop. I made 12 sleeves of wool. I am the 344
fastest sleeve cutter, so I get the best score, and I win." 356

Chee said, "Hold it. I cut 12 sleeves, too." 365

The others said that the score was the same for each dog. 377
Rop was getting madder and madder. He said, "This meet has 388
not ended yet." 391

Rop said, "We will see which of us is the best at tricking the 405
other one. The first dog to get the other dog to say, 'I do,' wins." 420

Chee said, "This is going to be easy. Ho, ho, hee, hee, hep. 433
You don't know how to make anybody say that." 442

[2]

Rop got really mad. He said, "Oh, yes I do." 452

"You said, 'I do,' " Chee said. 458

One worker said, "Chee wins the meet." 465

Another worker said, "Chee and Rop are very good. It is a 477
shame that they cannot be pals." 483

Rop said, "Who said we can't be pals? If we wish to be pals, 497
we will be pals." 501

"That is the way I see it," Chee said. 510

From that day on, Chee worked in the sleeve plant. And 521
Chee became pals with Rop. 526

Rop did not yell at Chee, and Chee did not holler at Rop. 539
They were the best of pals. 545

[1]

Lesson 38

1

dock sold more sailor steel drained

shore beach thin float nail story

2

A	B
your	yourself
seven	seventeen
an	another
some	someone
can	cannot

3

close to lake holes blade

waves while nose side

4

Japan coming turn water

ready ramp slow any

bottom left think from

fog sink swim board

women woman know

Lesson 38

5

Sink That Ship

Kit made a boat. She made the boat of tin. The nose of the 14
boat was very thin. Kit said, "I think that this boat is ready for 28
me to take on the lake." So Kit went to the lake with her boat. 43

Her boat was a lot of fun. It went fast. But when she went to 58
dock it at the boat ramp, she did not slow it down. And the 72
thin nose of the boat cut a <u>hole</u> in the boat ramp. 84

The man who sold gas at the boat ramp got mad. He said, 97
"That boat cuts like a blade. Do not take the boat on this lake 111
any more. Take it where you will not run into things." 122

[1]

So Kit did not take her boat to the lake any more. She went 136
to the sea with her boat. She said, "There is a lot of room in the 152
sea. I will not run this boat into any docks." 162

So Kit went on the sea with her boat. The nose of her boat 176
went into the waves like a blade. Kit's boat went faster and 188
faster. She said, "I am a good sailor." 196

After a while, she did not see the shore of the sea any more. 210
So Kit went to the left. She said, "I think this is the way back 225
to shore." But now the boat was on its way to Japan. 237

[1]

A thick fog came in. Kit did not see a thing. She said, "I 251
think I hear waves on the shore." 258

But Kit did not hear waves on the shore. The waves were 270
coming from the nose of a big ship. That big ship was very near 284
Kit's thin boat. Kit said, "I do hear waves. I must be near a beach." 299

Just then, a big ship came out of the fog. Kit's thin boat was 313
close to that ship. Kit said, "It is time to turn." 324

Kit turned the wheel of her boat, but the boat did not turn fast. 338
[1]

The thin nose of Kit's boat went into the steel side of the big 352
ship. The thin nose cut a hole in the ship. 362

The women and men on the deck of the ship yelled at Kit, 375
"Stop that, or you will sink this big ship." 384

Kit said, "I cannot stop. I think my boat likes to cut holes in 398
things." 399

And Kit's boat cut the biggest hole you have ever seen. The 411
sea began to run into that hole. And the big ship began to sink. 425
The people yelled, "Jump from the side of the ship." 435

"Swim to my boat," Kit said. And the people did. Seventeen 446
men, 47 women, three dogs, and a pet goat got on Kit's boat. 459
[1]

An old woman said, "This boat cannot float with all of these 471
people on board." 474

Just then, the sea began to run over the side of the boat. Kit 488
said, "I can stop this boat from sinking." 496

She got a hammer and a nail. She held the nail in her left 510
hand and gave it a rap with the hammer. She made a hole in 524
the bottom of the boat. Then she made another hole and 535
another hole. 537

"What are you doing?" the others asked. 544

Kit said, "I made holes in the bottom of the boat to drain 557
the water from this boat." 562

Do you think the water drained from the boat? 571

You will see in the next story. 578
[2]

Lesson 39

1

goat drain tools shut shore

yum rushed cheered reach

2

A	B
every	everybody
any	anyone
some	somebody
down	downhill

3

holes these likes safe while take

4

head won't melon again middle

bottom water coming bigger

wool filled patted you'll out

sniffed chomp sailor's easy

turn steered ordered sleeve

5

The Goat and Kit's Boat

Kit's boat was in the middle of the sea. It had made a hole in 15
a big ship. The big ship went down. Seventeen men, 47 women, 27
three dogs, and a pet goat got in Kit's boat. So Kit made holes 41
in the bottom of the boat to drain the water from the boat. 54

And the water did begin to drain, but not very fast. Kit said, 67
"These holes are not letting water out faster than water is 78
coming in the boat. We need a bigger hole in the bottom." 90

A sailor said, "We left our tools on board the big ship, so we 104
have no way to make bigger holes." 111

[1]

A man said, "So let's just yell for help. HELP, HELP." 122

"Hush up," Kit said. "We will get back to shore if we just 135
keep our heads and think of a way to make a big hole that will 150
drain water very fast." 154

An old woman said, "My pet goat likes to eat tin. Maybe he 167
can eat a hole in the bottom of this tin boat." 178

"Yes," Kit said. "Let's see what that goat can do." Then she 190
ordered everybody to make room for the goat to eat. "Eat," Kit 202
said. 203

[1]

And the goat did begin to eat, but it didn't eat the tin boat. It 218
ate a man's wool sleeve. "Stop that," he yelled. "Eat tin, not wool." 231

Kit said, "Yes, don't let that goat get filled up on wool. It 244
won't have any room for tin." 250

The old woman who had the pet goat patted the bottom of 262
the tin boat and told the goat, "Yum, yum. Eat this. You'll like 275
it a lot." 278

The goat sniffed the bottom of the boat and then began to 290
chomp on a sailor's cap. "Take that cap away from the goat," 302
Kit said. 304

At last, the goat sniffed the bottom of the boat and began to 317
eat the tin. 320

[2]

Lesson 39

The goat made a little hole and kept on eating until that hole 333
was bigger than a melon. 338

The water rushed out of the boat, and everybody cheered. 348
"Let's hear it for the goat," somebody yelled. And everybody 358
cheered again. 360

Kit said, "There are 65 people in this little boat, and we are 373
safe. But now we must get back to shore." 382

"That's easy," a sailor said. "Just turn that way and you'll 393
reach shore in a little while." 399

So Kit steered the boat, and soon it came to the shore. 65 412
people, three dogs, and one pet goat stepped from the little 423
boat. And everybody was happy. 428

[2]

Lesson 40

1

story painted streak crunch path

smashed bank trench next speed

2

A	B
down	downhill
an	another
some	something
every	everybody

3

nine holes dime waves mile shape

4

front why through tossed asked don't

won't fixing turned leaving from ripping

head closer lower slower know water

5

Kit's Boat Goes Faster and Faster

This is another story about Kit and her tin boat. Kit had her 13
boat at the dock. She was fixing the hole that the goat made in 27
the boat. She painted her boat green. Then she asked the man 39
who sold gas at the dock, "Where can I get some big rocks?" 52

The man said, "Why do you need big rocks?" 61

Kit said, "I will drop them in the front of my boat." 73

The man asked, "Why will you do that?" 81

Kit said, "So that my boat will go faster. I don't like boats 94
that go slow." 97
[1]

The man said, "How will the rocks in the front of your boat 110
make the boat go faster?" 115

Kit said, "Don't you see? The rocks will make the front of 127
my boat lower than the back of my boat. So my boat will be 141
going downhill. Things go very fast when they go downhill." 151

The man said, "Ho, ho. Those rocks will just make your 162
boat go slower." 165

But Kit got rocks and dropped them in the front of her boat. 178
Then she said, "Now it is time to see how fast this boat will run." 193
[1]

The front of the boat was very low in the water. When Kit let go 208
of the rope, the boat began to go—faster and faster. It went over 222
the waves like a streak. It went faster than the big speed boats. It 236
went faster than any boat on the sea. But it began to turn to the 251
left. It turned more and more. Soon it was going for the dock. 264

The man on the dock said, "I'm leaving this dock." And he did. 277

Kit said, "I wish this boat didn't go so fast." 287

But the boat kept going faster. It came closer and closer to the 300
dock. And then—crunch!—it smashed the dock into little bits. 311
[1]

Kit said, "This boat does not stop on a dime. In fact, this 324
boat does not stop." The boat kept going. It cut a trench into 337
the side of a hill in back of the dock. It cut a path next to the 354
road. It made a hole in the side of a bank. 365

At last Kit said, "I think I can make this fast boat stop. I will 380
toss the rocks from the nose of the boat. Then the boat will not 394
be going downhill." 397

So she began to toss rocks from the boat's nose. She tossed 409
five rocks. Then she tossed another rock, but it was not a rock. 422
It was a bag of gold. 428

[2]

When the boat went through the bank, nine bags of gold fell 440
in the boat. Kit tossed them from the boat, and the boat 452
stopped. The boat was a mile from the bank. 461

Then a cop ran up to Kit. She said to Kit, "We have you 475
now, you bank robber." 479

Kit said, "I did not rob a bank." 487

The cop said, "Yes, you did. You made this sled for ripping 499
holes in banks." 502

Kit said, "I am in bad shape, but I think I can fix things." 516

In the next story, you will see what Kit did. 526

[1]

Lesson 41

1

leave floating sails reached splash shore

2

A	B
up	upside
paint	paintbrush
any	anything
some	somebody

3

why try fly sky

4

shape bribe crime smiled

dive sides bike pike white

5

goodbye light nothing bay yellow

front stepped slid slipped grinned

into fins turned open over

water through hollered herself

6

Kit Makes Her Boat Lighter

Kit was in bad shape. She said, "I can fix things up." 12

The cop said, "Do not try to bribe us. This is a crime." 25

Kit said to her, "I was not trying to bribe you. But you must 39
help me. I need yellow paint." 45

The cop said, "Why do you need yellow paint?" 54
Kit said, "Get me the paint, and you will see." 64
So the cop got another cop to run for the paint. The cop 77
stepped in front of Kit and said, "Do not try to leave." When the 91
other cop came back with the can of yellow paint, Kit smiled. 103
Then she took the lid from the can and began to paint her 116
boat yellow. 118

[1]

"What are you doing?" the cops asked. "How can it help 129
anything to paint that boat yellow?" 135
Kit grinned and said, "You will see." 142
Kit got in the boat, and the boat began to float up into the 156
sky. The cops said, "Do you see what I see? That boat is 169
floating in the sky." 173
Kit smiled. Then she hollered down to the cops, "Goodbye." 183
The cops hollered, "Why is that boat floating?" 191
Kit said, "You see, the boat was green, and now it is yellow. 204
Yellow is lighter than green. Now the boat is so light that it 217
floats in the sky." 221
The boat sailed over a town. Then it turned and sailed over 233
the bay. Then it began to sail over the open sea. 244

[2]

Kit smiled and said, "Now I will get my can of green paint 257
and make this boat green. Green is not as light as yellow, so 270
this boat will take a dive into the water." 279
So Kit reached over the side and began to paint. She painted 291
the sides of the boat green, but her paintbrush did not reach 303
the bottom of the boat. So the bottom of the boat was still 316
yellow. That made the bottom lighter than the sides. So the 327
boat turned over. 330

Lesson 41

Kit said, “I think I am going to take a dive into the sea.” 344
And she did. 347

Splash! 348

[1]

The boat slid into the water upside down. Kit said, “I will 360
flip this boat over and take it back to shore.” 370

She flipped it over. Then she got a grip on the rail. There was a 385
big pike in the bottom of the boat. The pike had yellow paint on 399
its back and on its sides. When the fish flipped its fins, it went into 414
the sky. The fish was very light. The pike floated over the town. 427

Kit said, “I am going to sell this boat and get a bike. This 441
boat is nothing but a pain.” 447

Then she said to herself, “I can have a lot of fun with a bike. 462
If I get a white bike, it will be very light, so I’ll fly over town.” 478

[2]

Lesson 42

1

wham shaft heap wait store

near boating stacks shelf chin

2

A	B
through	throughout
free	freeway
with	without
every	everything

3

while home here notes stroked taken

4

Henry motor words dragged

looked book rubbed fixed

why cam because work ever

don't how glasses picked my

nothing list front goodbye

opened dollars know lighter

5

Henry's Hot Rod

Henry had a hot rod. He ran his hot rod very fast down the 14
freeway. But he ran it too fast, and—wham!—there went his 26
cam shaft. Henry said, "Now my hot rod will not go." 37

Lesson 42

A truck came and dragged Henry's hot rod back to a motor 49
shop. The shop man looked at the motor. Then he rubbed his 61
chin. He said, "I don't think I can get to this job for three 75
weeks. When do you need this heap?" 82

Henry said, "That hot rod is not a heap. Why can't you get 95
to it now?" 98

The shop man rubbed his chin. Then he said, "I don't have 110
time." 111

[1]

The shop man said, "I have three other jobs. When I get 123
them fixed, I can work on your rod." 131

Henry said, "Where can I take my hot rod to get it fixed now?" 145

The shop man said, "There is no shop in town that can do 158
the work now. They have lots of jobs." 166

"Why is that?" Henry asked. 171

"Because people go too fast when they go down the 181
freeway," the shop man said. 186

Henry said, "I will not wait. I will fix my motor at home." 199

"That seems like the best thing to do," the shop man said. "I 212
can't do the job here, so why not do it at home?" 224

"That is what I will do," Henry said. 232

[1]

The shop man asked, "Have you ever fixed a motor?" 242

"No," Henry said. "But that will not stop me. I have looked 254
at my motor, and I don't see why I can't do the job." 267

The shop man told Henry, "You had better get a book that 279
tells how to fix motors." 284

"Yes," Henry said. 287

So the shop man had Henry's hot rod taken to Henry's home. Then Henry went to a book store. When he got there, he asked the woman in the store, "Where are the books on motors?"

[1]

The woman at the book store said, "The books on motors are over there, near the books on boating."

Henry looked at the stacks of books. But Henry did not know how to read. He said to the woman, "I do not have my glasses with me, and I cannot read without them. Can you help me get a book?"

The woman went to the shelf and picked up three books. She handed them to Henry. Then she said, "The green book is not bad. There are things in the red book that are very good. But a lot of people say that the yellow book is the best. It gives lots of notes on how to fix everything in a motor."

[2]

"Where are the notes on the cam shaft?" Henry asked.

The woman said, "There is a list in the front of the book. I'll check it." She did.

She opened the book and handed it to Henry. "Here is everything you need to know," she said.

Henry looked at the words, but he did not know how to read. He stroked his chin and looked at the book. Then he said, "Yes, this book is what I need."

So he gave the woman ten dollars and said, "Thank you." Then he went home with his book.

[1]

Lesson 43

1

bolts reader before steering clear

which roar wish belts tore

2

A	B
make	making
dive	diving
trade	trading
smile	smiling
smoke	smoking

3

A	B
him	himself
door	doorway
every	everything

4

Molly foot saw does whisper again

motors why fixing press seals words

lifted know means tossed book some

strip rested bottom steel through

5

Henry's Sister Helps Him

Henry got a book on fixing motors. Henry went home with 11
the book. He sat in his hot rod and looked at the words in the 26
book, but Henry did not know how to read those words. 37

Here is what it said in the book: "There are three bolts that 50
hold this end of the cam shaft." 57

Here is what Henry was reading: "Where are there belts that 68
hold this end for a came shaft." 75

Henry said, "What does that mean?" 81

He kept reading. Here is what it said in his book: "When you 94
take the seals from the shaft, you press on them and then lift 107
them from the shaft." 111

[1]

This is what Henry said when he was reading those words: 122
"Why take and steal I dress and then lifted them of the shaft." 135

Henry said, "I don't know what this book means." He tossed 146
the book down and said, "I don't need a book to fix this motor. 160
I have seen people work on motors, and I don't think it will be 174
a very big job." 178

So Henry began to work on his motor. While he was taking 190
some bolts from the motor, a flat strip fell on his foot. "Ow!" he 204
yelled. 205

[1]

Then he took some other bolts from the motor, and the 216
motor fell on his foot. "Ow," he yelled. He jumped up and 228
down and yelled some more. 233

His sister, Molly, came through the doorway. "What did you 243
do?" Molly asked. "Why are you yelling?" 250

"My foot," he yelled. "That motor fell on my foot." 260
Molly said, "I don't think you know what you are doing. Did 272
you read a book before you began to work on your hot rod?" 285
"That book does not make sense," Henry said. 293
Molly got the book and sat next to Henry in his hot rod. She 307
rested the book on the steering wheel. Then she said, "This 318
book seems very clear to me." 324

[2]

"Will you read it to me?" Henry asked. 332
"Why not?" Molly said. Then she began to read. "When you 343
work on the cam shaft, take out the 15 bolts from the pan of 357
the motor." 359
"Where is the pan?" Henry asked. 365
"I will read and see," his sister said. Molly began to read 377
again. "The pan is on the bottom of the motor. To reach the 390
cam shaft, you must take the pan from the motor." 400
So Henry took the bolts from the pan. When he had taken 412
the pan from the motor, he saw that there were lots of steel 425
things that made the motor work. 431

[1]

Henry said to Molly, "Does the book tell which of these 442
things is the cam shaft?" 447
She said, "I don't know, and I have to go to work. Here is the 462
book. It tells where everything is on the motor. Read the book, 474
and it will tell you what you need to know." 484
So Molly went to the street and jumped into her hot rod. She 497
grabbed the wheel, and—roar—she tore down the street. 507
Henry took his book and whispered to himself, "I wish I was 519
a better reader." 522

[1]

1

dinner shaft gear each

bolted stick steel

2

file these pile taken

those while broken

3

A	B
time	timing
smoke	smoking
take	taking
ride	riding

4

A	B
in	inside
my	myself
home	homework

5

clothes done aside together Henry

Molly trying motors tossed turn

dragging wham I've foot front their

fixed saying saw know slipped

took does again flying believe you're

6

Molly Fixes Her Hot Rod

Henry was trying to fix his motor, but he was not doing very 13
well. He was looking at the words in his book on motors, but 26
Henry did not know what they said. The book said: "To turn a 39
cam shaft, you file each cam." 45

But this is what Henry said as he was reading: "To turn a 58
cam shaft, you fill each cam." 64

Henry said, "What does that mean?" He tossed the book 74
aside and said, "That book is not helping me very much. I can 87
do the job myself." So Henry worked and worked. 96

[1]

After a while, his motor was in little bits. Now he did not 109
have a motor. He had a heap of steel. 118

"Where is the cam shaft?" he asked as he looked at the big 131
pile of steel. 134

He picked up a big gear. "Is this a cam shaft?" he asked. He 148
ran his hand over the teeth of the gear. "These things must be 161
the cams," he said. 165

Henry was looking at the gear when a truck came down the 177
street. The truck was dragging his sister's hot rod. 186

Molly was mad. She ran over to Henry and said, "Where is 198
that book? My motor broke down, and I've got to fix it fast." 211

[2]

Molly grabbed the book. She ran to her hot rod and began 223
to work. 225

When it was time for dinner, Molly had fixed her hot rod. 237
She had taken the pan from the motor. She had taken three 249
bent rods from the motor. She had taken those rods to a shop 262

where they were fixed. Then she had slipped them back into the 274
motor and bolted them on the pan. 281

While she was doing this, Henry was still looking at the gear. 293
He kept saying, "This must be the cam shaft," but he didn't 305
know what to do with it. 311

[1]

Henry didn't know where the gear came from or how to stick 323
it back into his motor. He didn't even know why the motor 335
needed the gear. 338

Molly slipped into some clean clothes, ate dinner, and took 348
off in her hot rod. Henry began to bolt his motor back 360
together. When he was done, he said, "There are bits of steel 372
that are left over." 376

He had a gear, a wheel, three rods, and some little bolts. 388

"Well," he said, "I think this motor will work well now." 399

[1]

His hot rod did not run. Bits of steel went flying this way and 413
that way. Smoke came from the motor. Then the motor fell 424
from the hot rod. 428

Molly had just come home. She said, "I can't believe this 439
mess." 440

Henry asked, "Will you help me fix my motor?" 449

"No," she said. "I must do my homework for school. Read 460
your book, and you can fix it." 467

"But I can't read," Henry said. "You'll have to read to me." 479

"Not me," she said. Molly went inside. Henry sat looking at 490
his smoking motor. He was very, very sad. 498

[1]

Lesson 45

1

rid con paths trenches tore seems

grip fishing think west tin aim

2

A	B
him	himself
some	someone
be	become
every	everybody

3

holes crime grips traded tires site

pike fine these hike later fishing

4

ripped robber rested out began

clock cash black before happen

ready done biggest together

5

Kit's Trade

Kit said, "I think I will get rid of this boat. It makes ships 14
sink. It has ripped up 2 docks. It has made paths and trenches. 27
It tore holes in the bank, and that is a bad crime." 39

Kit had a lot to gripe over. So she said, "I will sell the boat." 54
She made a note and stuck it on the side of the tin boat. The 69
note said: 71

FOR SALE. A TIN BOAT 76
I WILL TRADE FOR A BIKE. 82

The con man was in town. He had five tires. Each tire had a 96
hole in it. 99

[1]

The con man said, "I will sit at this site until I see someone 113
to con." So he sat down on the tires. He was very tired. 126

While he rested, Kit came up the dock. The con man said to 139
himself, "If I can con this woman, I can get rid of my tires. 153
Then I will get some pike to eat. I like fish." 164

The con man said, "I have some fine tires if you have 176
something to trade." 179

Kit said, "I have a boat to trade, but I don't like to trade for 194
tires. I need a bike." 199

[1]

The con man said, "Trade your boat for these tires. Then 210
you can take these tires and trade them for a bike." 221

Kit said, "That seems like a good thing to do." 231

The con man said, "Get a grip on these tires, and let's hike 244
down to your boat." So Kit grabbed the tires, and she went 256
with the con man to the boat. 263

The con man stopped near the boat. He said, "I will not trade 276
five fine tires for this tin heap. I will trade you for three tires." 290

Kit said, "But this boat is a fine fishing boat. And it will go 304
fast if you drop rocks in the nose." 312

[1]

Kit told the con man how fast the boat went with the rocks 325
in the nose. She told the con man how the boat went into the 339
bank and came out with nine bags of gold. 348

The con man began to think this: "I will get the boat, and I 362
will fill the nose with rocks. Then I will become the best bank 375
robber in the West." 379

Lesson 45

But Kit said, "No, I don't think I will trade this boat for the 393
tires. I need a bike." 398
The con man said, "I will let you have these five fine tires. 411
And I will give you my clock, my cash, and my gold ring." 424

[2]

So Kit and the con man traded. And later Kit traded the 436
gold ring for a black bike. 442
The con man got heaps of rocks and dropped them in the 454
nose of the boat. He said, "Now I am ready to become the best 468
bank robber in the West. When the sun comes up in the east, I 482
will aim the boat at the biggest bank in town. Before the day is 496
over, I will have heaps of gold." 503
When you read the next story, you will see what happens to 515
the con man. 518

[1]

Lesson 46

1

heap deep flash trench

rocket diver float leave

2

space idea covered seconds air

seal tug where ready water

began bits does because

3

light mile smile taffy

bribe sink sea gripping

faster fastest bottom lifted

waves spray flying zipped

lint skin cotton under

4

The Con Man Gets Cotton Taffy Pike

The con man had traded his clock, his cash, his ring, and 12
five tires with holes in them for Kit's tin boat. 22

Now the con man was ready to become the best bank robber 34
in the West. He said, "I will pile rocks in the nose of this boat. 49
The more rocks I pile, the faster it will go. So I will make this 64
boat the fastest thing there is." 70

So the con man slid the boat into deep water near the dock. 83
Then the con man got a big pile of rocks. He dropped ten rocks 97
into the nose of the boat. Then he dropped ten more. 108

[1]

Lesson 46

He said, “Now this boat will go very fast.” The nose of the 121
boat was low in the water. 127

The con man heaped ten more rocks into the nose of the 139
boat. Then he said, “Now this boat will . . . sink.” And it did. 151
The nose of the boat went down. And “glub, blub,” the boat 163
went to the bottom of the sea. 170

The con man made a deal with a skin diver. The con man 183
gave the skin diver a coat. 189

[1]

The skin diver went under the water and lifted the pile of 201
rocks from the boat. Then the boat began to float. 211

The con man said, “This time, I will not heap so many rocks 224
in the nose of this boat.” So the con man dropped six rocks 237
into the nose. He hopped into the boat and said, “Now I will 250
fly over the waves.” 254

But the boat did not fly over the waves. It did not go as fast 269
as a sick pike. A seal passed the con man in the water. A tug 284
boat passed him. So did a woman in a row boat. 295

The con man began to gripe. “Bad, bad,” he said. “This boat 307
will not go a mile in a year.” 315

[2]

He picked up the paddle and went back to the dock. He 327
heaped ten more rocks in the nose. Then the boat went like a 340
flash. It cut a hole in the water and sent spray flying 600 feet in 355
the air. It went a mile in three seconds. 364

The con man began to smile. “Now I will rip into the biggest 377
bank in town,” he said. 382

The con man turned the boat and went for shore. He was not 395
griping now. He was grinning. And he was gripping the wheel 406

with his hands. He was thinking, "I will slide into that bank 418
and get rich." 421

[2]

The boat smashed into a dock and tore it to bits. Then it 434
went up the beach. It cut a trench up the hill. It was going as 449
fast as a rocket. The con man said, "I can't tell where the bank 463
is." 464

Before he had time to think, the boat ripped into the side of 477
a fish-packing plant. The boat made a hole in the other side of 490
the plant. But the con man did not have bags of gold in the 504
boat. He had piles of striped pike. He said, "These fish stink." 516

[1]

Before he had time to think, the boat ripped into the side of 529
a taffy plant. Now the con man had sticky taffy. And he had a 543
boat filled with taffy pike. 548

The boat tore a hole into a cotton mill. When it zipped from 561
the mill, the con man had bits of cotton lint on his taffy. He 575
had cotton taffy pike. 579

The con man said, "I must leave this town and hide from the 592
cops. But I cannot steer this boat. What will I do?" 603

What do you think he will do? 610

[1]

Lesson 47

1

heaving wheel smashed

their hollered jail

2

A	B
some	somewhere
any	anything
every	everybody
boat	boatload

3

sticking must slid stared tossing

taffy cotton pants scare sticky factory

striped press mill steering hide lint

began come space covered idea light

4

A Thing from Space

The con man was zipping here and there in Kit's tin boat. 12
The boat went into a fish-packing plant, into a taffy plant, and 24
into a cotton mill. The con man was a mess. He had a mess of 39
cotton taffy pike in his boat. The steering wheel had taffy on it. 52

The con man said, "I must go somewhere and hide. I must 64
throw the rocks out of this boat so that it will slow down." 77

[1]

He began tossing cotton taffy rocks from the nose of the 88
boat. The boat went slower and slower. Then the con man 99

began heaving the pile of pike from the boat. Soon the main 111
street of the town had cotton taffy on it. The boat began to 124
slow down. 126

The con man said, "Now I will run and hide before the cops 139
come here." But when he went to slip from the boat, he said, "I 153
am sticking to the seat. This taffy will not let go of me." 166

[1]

The cops and their nine dogs ran up to the con man. The 179
man from the dock ran up to him. The man hollered, "That is 192
the man who smashed my dock into bits." 200

The woman from the fish-packing plant ran up to the con 211
man. The fish packer said, "That is the man who made a hole 224
in my plant. He zipped away with a boatload of striped pike." 236

The man from the taffy factory came running up the street. 247
He yelled, "Stop that man. He tore a hole in my plant and stole 261
a boatload of taffy." 265

[2]

The woman who ran the cotton mill was next. She was really 277
mad. She said, "This is the man who broke my cotton-making 288
press." 289

The cops yelled, "We have you now. We will send you to jail 302
for the rest of your life." 308

The dogs said, "Ooowww, ooowww." 313

The con man said, "Bad, bad. I don't like jails. I must get out 327
of here fast." 330

Then the con man got an idea. He said to himself, "I must 343
look funny. I am covered with cotton lint." 351

Slowly the con man began to stand up. The taffy was 362
sticking to his pants, and he had torn a big hole in his pants. 376

The con man said, "Do not bother me. This is a space ship. 388
And I come from space." 393

[2]

The dogs stopped going, "Ooowww." The cops stopped 401
running. The other people stopped hollering. They stared at 410
the con man. Then the woman from the cotton mill said, "It 422
must be from space. I have never seen anything like it before." 434

The man from the dock said, "It is more like a bag of cotton 448
than anything I have seen." 453

The man from the taffy plant said, "I am leaving. I don't 465
think I like things from space." 471

The con man said to himself, "Ho, ho. They think that I am 484
from space. I think I will scare them. Ho, ho." 494

What do you think the con man will do next? 504

[2]

Lesson 48

1

near rain what gold

leave splash drain before

2

A	B
every	everybody
an	another
every	everything
him	himself

3

sticking melt fate teller safe

scare smashed striped lint cotton

middle didn't plop before hospital

skin robbery spot pick space

light nose idea covered

4

The Bank Robbery Fails

The con man made everybody think that he was from space. 11
He was a big mass of cotton lint. The cotton lint was sticking 24
to the taffy. And the taffy was sticking to the con man's skin. It 38
was sticking to everything. The con man said to himself, "I will 50
give these people the scare of their lives." 58

He held up his hands and said a deep "Rrrrr." 68

Three dogs went, "Ooowww," and ran down the street. 77

Then the con man said, "I am from space, and I will get you." 91

The dock man said, "I'm going to run to the sea and dive 104
in." That is what he did. So did the people from the plants. 117

[2]

The cops said, "Let's not make this space thing mad." They 128
smiled at him. 131

The con man said, "Rrrrr. I will get you." He began to go for 145
the cops. 147

The cops said, "We had better leave this spot." And they did. 159
They ran down the street and—splash!—they dived into the sea. 171

The con man was standing in the middle of the street. 182
Nobody was near him. He said, "Wow! This is fun. I think I'll 195
go into the bank and see if I can pick up some bags of gold." 210

[1]

The con man said, "I will go into the bank." The con man 223
didn't see well. His nose was a mass of cotton lint. So the con 237
man didn't see a striped pike in front of the bank. 248

Slip! There went the con man when he stepped on the pike. 260
Plop! That was the con man hitting the street with his seat. 272

"Bad, bad," the con man griped. He picked up the striped 283
pike and flipped it into the street. Then he went into the bank. 296

He went up to the teller in the bank. The con man said to 310
her, "Rrrrr. I am a space man, and I need gold." 321

[2]

The teller said, "Take the gold you want from the safe and 333
leave." 334

So the con man took some gold. Then he took more gold. He 347
said, "Now I have more gold than I can hold." 357

He lifted three big bags of gold and left the bank. He went 370
into the street. He did not see the striped pike in the middle of 384
the street. 386

Slip! That was the con man. Plop! That was the con man's 398
seat hitting the street. Plop, plop, plop! Those were the bags of 410
gold landing on the con man. 416

[1]

"Bad, bad," the con man griped. He grabbed the bags and 427
began to stand up. But just then a drop of rain hit the con man 442
on the hand. Then another drop landed on his coat. Then five 454
more hit him. The con man said, "I must hide before the rain 467
makes me wet. If I get wet, the taffy will melt. Then the lint 481
will not stick. And then everybody will see that I am not from 494
space. They will see that I am the con man." 504

The con man began to run with the bags of gold. But the 517
bags were not light, and the con man did not run very fast. He 531
said, "Bad, bad. This rain is making my plan go down the 543
drain." 544

[2]

Lesson
49

1

sore moaned what

raining sneak licked jailer

2

laugh walk hair plop landed

idea space bank pale coming

3

busted liked taffy trick slide

three slippery trying dying tired

4

The Con Man Gets Busted

It was raining, and the con man was griping about the rain. 12
He said, "My plan is going down the drain." 21

He was trying to run with the three bags of gold, but they 34
were not light, and he did not run fast. The cotton in his hair 48
was running down his nose. He did not see where he was going. 61
He slipped on a pile of slippery pike and—plop, plop, plop!— 73
the con man hit the street, and the three bags of gold landed on 87
the con man. 90

[1]

A little boy was standing near the con man. The boy said, 102
"You are not from space. I can see that you are just a wet man." 117

The lint was sliding from the con man's hair, from his hands, 129
from his nose, and from his coat. The rain was coming down 141
very fast, and the con man was very, very wet. 151

A dog ran up to the con man and began to lick the taffy 165
from his hand. “Don’t bite me,” the con man said. And the dog 178
did not bite. It licked and licked. It liked the taffy. Then three 191
cats came up to the con man. They began to lick the taffy. 204

[2]

Then five dogs and nine goats came over and began licking 215
taffy. 216

“I don’t like this,” the con man said. He was trying to get up. 230
He said, “I must get to the other side of the street.” But he 244
slipped on a striped pike and—plop!—he was back on his seat 257
in the street. 260

The cops ran up to the con man. “Don’t try to leave,” they 273
said. “We’ve got you now, you slippery sneak.” 281

“Ooowww,” the con man moaned. “Now I will have to go 292
to jail.” 294

[1]

And that is just what happened. The cops and nine dogs led 306
the con man to the jail. They locked the con man up. Then 319
they sent the gold back to the bank. 327

The con man said, “I hate jails. I must get out of here.” He 341
began to think of ways to trick the cops into letting him go. 354

Then he got an idea. He began moaning, “Oh, oh. I am sick. 367
I am pale. I am not well.” 374

The jailer came to the other side of the door. She said, “If 387
you are sick, we will have to send you to the hospital.” 399

“Yes, yes,” the con man said. “I think I am dying. That’s 411
how sick I am.” 415

[2]

The jailer yelled for a cop. “Get this man to the hospital,” 427
she said. 429

The cop said, “Do you think this man is faking?” 439

“No,” the jailer said. “This man is very cold. And he seems 451
to be very pale. I don’t think he is faking. I think he’s sick.” 465

The con man was smiling to himself. He was thinking, “I 476
may seem sick, but I am still in fine shape for conning jailers.” 489

So the jailer opened the door, and the cop said, “Well, if he’s 502
not acting, we had better take him to the hospital.” 512

You will see what happened when you read the next con 523
man story. 525

[2]

Lesson 50

1

leaves shade holes sneak

wish waited creep lower hear

2

buy walked find bend luck drum

here happy mother brothers come

3

anything sisters digging mine

joke came laugh hotter dusty

runner silver stayed

4

The Bug That Dug

There was a bug. That bug liked to dig. He dug and dug. His 14
mother said, "Why do you keep digging? The rest of us bugs 26
eat leaves and sit in the shade. But you dig and dig." 38

"When I dig, I feel happy," the digging bug said. "I like to 51
make holes." 53

So he made holes. When he stopped digging, he was dusty. 64
His brothers and sisters said, "You are a mess. You have dust 76
on your back. What are you doing?" 83

The bug said, "When I dig, I feel happy." And so that bug 96
dug and dug. 99

[1]

Then something happened. The days began to get hotter and 109
hotter. The sun was so hot that the other bugs said, "We 121
cannot stay here. It is too hot. We must go to a spot that is not 137
so hot." 139

They walked here and there, but they did not find a spot that 152
felt cool. Then they came to a big hole in the side of a hill. They 168
said, "Let's go down this hole. It looks cool inside." 178

The bugs went inside the hole. Then the mother bug stopped. 189
She said, "Did you hear that? I hear something in this hole." 201

The other bugs stopped. Then one of them said, "Yes, I hear 213
something. I think I hear digging." 219

[2]

So the bugs began to sneak down the hole. Soon they came 231
to a bend in the hole. The mother bug said, "Stay here, and I 245
will check out the digging." The other bugs waited, and the 256
mother bug began to creep to the bend. Then she stopped. 267

What do you think she saw? She saw a dusty bug digging 279
and digging. She said, "So this is where you go when you dig." 292

The dusty bug stopped digging. He said, "Yes, this is my 303
mine. I come here to dig every day." 311

[1]

"What are you digging for?" the mother bug asked. 320

"I mine gold," the bug said. 326

The mother bug began to laugh. She laughed and laughed. 336
She said, "That is a joke. A bug digging for gold. Did you ever 350
hear anything so funny?" 354

The dusty bug said, "Don't make fun of my gold mine. If I 367
don't find gold in this hole, I will get some silver." 378

"Silver," the mother bug said and began to laugh again. 388
When she stopped laughing, she said, "There is no silver in 399
these hills." 401

[1]

The bug said, "I'll bet you that I will have some silver before 414
the sun sets." 417

"That is a bet," his mother said. "This mine is a dud. I'll bet you a dollar that you won't have silver before the sun sets."

Then the dusty bug began to scream, "Leave this mine. I did not ask you to come here. So get out."

He ran to the other bugs. "Go home," he said. "Leave this mine."

But the other bugs said, "No. It is too hot in the sun. We like it here where it is cool."

[1]

The dusty bug said, "Pay me a dime, or leave my mine."

So each of the bugs gave the dusty bug a dime. Then the dusty bug went to the mother bug. He said, "When we bet, you said that I will not have silver when the sun sets, but I have lots of silver in my hand."

The mother bug was mad, but she said, "You win." She gave him a dollar.

But then the dusty bug said, "Now you must pay a dime if you wish to stay in my mine." So the mother bug gave the dusty bug a dime.

The bugs stayed in that mine until the sun was lower and the air was not so hot.

[2]

Lesson 51

1

ou

A	B
out	sound
our	mouth
loud	outside

2

gone clerk burp cash one buy

smell walk such tired door

another laugh handed rotten

side joking rusty eating

grinned chomp three smiled

3

The Bug and the Pickle Tub

The dusty bug was resting in his mine. It was hot outside. He 13
had a rusty shovel. He had been digging with the shovel, but 25
now he was tired. He said, "I need to eat. I like dill pickles, but 40
I don't have any dills." 45

He tossed the shovel to one side. Then he came out of his 58
mine. The sun was very hot. The bug went to a store. Then he 72
picked up a tub of pickles. He said to the clerk, "Will you bill 86
me for these dill pickles?" 91

The clerk said, "No, we do not bill for pickles. You must pay 104
cash in this store." 108

[1]

The bug said, "I don't have cash with me. But if you send me 122
a bill, I will pay for it." 129
The clerk said, "You did not hear me. I said that we do not 143
bill for dill pickles." 147
The bug said, "That's fine with me. Now that I smell these 159
pickles, I can tell that they are rotten." 167
"They are not rotten," the clerk said. "They are the best 178
pickles in town." 181
The bug began to laugh. Then he said, "These pickles are so 193
bad that they will make you sick if you eat them." 204

[1]

The clerk ran over to the bug. The clerk said, "Give me one 217
of those pickles. I'll show you that they are good." 227
The bug handed the pickle to the clerk. The clerk chomped 238
on the pickle. Then the clerk smiled. "That dill is fine," she said. 251
The bug said, "You must have picked a good dill, but some 263
of these dills are bad." The bug picked up a big dill and began 277
to chomp on it. He puckered his mouth. Then he said, "That 289
dill is bad." 292

[1]

The clerk reached into the pickle tub and got a big pickle. 304
She ate it in three chomps. Then she grinned. "My, my," she 316
said. "That was a good pickle. In fact, that was the best dill I 330
have had in some time." 335
The bug dug into the tub and got a big dill. He chomped it 349
down. Then he said, "That dill was a dud. It was so bad that I 364
feel sick." 366

Lesson 51

The clerk said, "You don't know a good dill when you eat 378
one." So the clerk dug a big dill from the tub. She smelled it. 392
"Good, good," she said. Then she ate it. 400

[1]

When the clerk was done eating, she said, "My, my, did you 412
ever see such a good dill?" 418

The dusty bug said, "I think you are joking. You say that the 431
dills are good, but the dills that I eat are bad." 442

The clerk dug another dill from the tub. She handed it to the 455
bug and said, "Try this dill. It is not a dud. I'll tell you that." 470

So the bug ate the dill. Then he smiled. He said, "You are 483
right. That dill is just fine. See if you can give me another one 497
that is good." 500

"That's easy," the clerk said. She got another dill and handed 511
it to the bug. The bug chomped it down. 520

[2]

Then the bug said, "You're good at digging out the best dills. 532
That dill was the best yet. See if you dig out another good one." 546

Soon the bug had eaten every pickle in the tub. Then he said, 559
"Well, I think I'll go back to my mine. I don't think I'll buy any 574
pickles today. So you don't have to send me a bill." 585

The clerk looked at the bug. Then she looked at the tub. She 598
said, "What is this? The dills are gone." 606

The dusty bug smiled from the door of the store. Then he 618
said, "Burp." And he went back to his mine. 627

[2]

1

ou

A	B
sound	mouth
hour	house
found	outside
cloud	loudly

2

orange floor eleven home hear rip

tug bing dinging bop bus

dropped wife liked woman before

clock deer cheer drink tape

saying maker didn't fixing bay

bees holding speak really gone

3

The Old Clock Maker

The old clock maker liked to work with plants when he 11
wasn't working with clocks. He had lots of plants in back of his 24
home. Every day after work, he dressed in a bib and went to 37
dabble with his plants. While he dabbled, he talked. He didn't 48
hear himself, so he didn't know that he was saying things very 60
loudly. When he came to a plant that did not have buds, he 73
said, "This plant is a dud because it doesn't have one bud." 85

[1]

One day, he was dabbling and talking when his wife came 96
out. She said, "A woman is here. Can you make a bid on fixing 110
a clock?" 112

The old clock maker did not hear her. The clock maker said, 124
"I do not have a rip in my bib." 133

His wife said, "I did not say 'bib,' I said 'bid.' A woman 146
needs a bid. Can you tell her how much she will have to pay?" 160

"I'm not going to the bay," the clock maker said. "I'm going 172
to stay here with the bees and my plants." 181

"Come with me," his wife said. "I will let you speak to the 194
woman." So she led the old clock maker inside. 203

[2]

A woman was standing near the door. She was holding a big 215
clock. The woman said, "When this clock works, a deer runs 226
out every hour, and the clock goes, 'ding, ding.' But the clock 238
does not work. The deer does not come out, and the clock goes, 251
'bing, bing.' " 253

The clock maker said, "I'm glad to meet you, Mrs. Bing 264
Bing. What can I do for you?" 271

The clock maker's wife said to the woman, "You will have to 283
yell if you want him to hear what you say." 293

So the woman yelled. She told the clock maker about the 304
deer and about the dinging and binging. 311

[1]

The clock maker said, "I've never seen a clock that cheered 322
every hour. I've seen clocks with a deer that comes out every 334
hour, but never a clock that cheers." 341

"No, no," the woman yelled. "This clock has a deer." 351

The clock maker said, "How does that work? Does the deer 362
make a cheer?" 365

The woman yelled, "There is no cheer, just a deer."

"Oh," the clock maker said.

[1]

The clock maker took off his big bib. Then he said, "When did the clock stop working?"

The woman yelled, "When I dropped it."

The clock maker said, "You must not bop clocks. The clock is a dud now."

"I didn't bop it," the woman yelled. "I dropped it. Drop, drop, drop."

The clock maker said, "So your clock has a leak, and it goes, 'drop, drop, drop.' Take a bit of tape and dab it on the hole. That will stop the leak."

"No," the woman yelled. "My clock does not leak. It is a bad clock. It doesn't work."

"Let me see that clock," the clock maker said.

[2]

He grabbed the clock and dropped it. The clock made a loud sound when it hit the floor. The deer fell out. A spring went, "bop." The clock went, "bing, bing, ding."

The clock maker said, "That clock is broken. Let me make a bid on fixing it for you."

The woman was really mad. She said, "You dropped that clock. It was not in such bad shape before you did that."

The clock maker said, "I will fix the clock for eleven dollars."

The woman said, "Good."

[1]

Lesson 53

1

house brush room deer

sound dear loudly paint dingers

2

parts girl held dong ding

fine well orange floor

3

working can't gone again

bobbed dabbed slapped frog

hands din miles room

fellow yellow looked himself

wiped why dear stand

4

The Deer That Bobbed Like a Frog

The clock maker gave a bid on the clock that he had 12
dropped. He made a bid of eleven dollars. Then he took the 24
clock to his work room. In that room he had lots of clocks. 37
Every hour, the clocks went, "dong, dong," and, "ding, ding." 47
But the clock maker did not hear them. 55

In the work room, the clock maker had a bin of parts from 68
other clocks. He also had a lot of tools for fixing clocks. 80

The clock maker held the clock with the deer. He said, "I 92
will have to paint this clock." So he got a brush and dabbed 105
paint on the clock. 109

[1]

He made the clock orange. Then he dabbed paint on the 120
deer. He made the deer yellow. 126

Then he went to his bin of old clocks to look for one that 140
had a good deer. He looked and looked. Then he began to talk 153
to himself. He said, "This is bad. I made a bid on fixing this 167
clock, but I cannot see another clock with a working deer. The 179
best I can see is a clock with a working frog. That frog comes 193
out every hour and bobs up and down." 201

The clock maker took the parts from the clock with the frog 213
and slapped them into the clock with the deer. 222

[2]

At the end of an hour, the deer came out and bobbed up and 236
down like a frog. The clock maker was happy. 245

Next the clock maker said, "Now I will fix the clock so that 258
it goes, 'ding, ding.' " 262

Five clocks in his bin had good dingers, but the clock maker 274
did not hear the sounds they made. He picked a clock that did 287
not go, "ding." That clock went, "dong, dong." 295

[1]

He took the bell from the clock that went "dong." He said, 307
"This part will work fine in the clock with a deer." So he 320
slapped the bell into the deer clock. Then he said, "Now the 332
woman will have a clock that works well." 340

The clock maker wiped his hands on his bib. Then he took 352
the clock to the woman. He said, "Here it is." 362

The woman looked at the clock. Just then, the bell went, 373
"dong, dong." The woman said, "What a sound! You can hear 384
this clock for miles." 388

Then the deer came out of the clock. 396

[2]

Lesson 53

The woman said, "What is that deer doing? It is bobbing up 408
and down like a frog. Why is this clock orange? And why is the 422
deer yellow?" 424

"Yes," the clock maker said. "He is a dear fellow." 434

"Not fellow," the woman said. "Yellow. Yellow. Why is it 444
yellow?" 445

"You don't have to yell," the clock maker said. "I can hear 457
you. I like it yellow, too." 463

The woman got so mad that she began to yell. "This clock 475
looks bad. When you gave a bid, you said, 'I will fix the clock.' 489
But now this clock is a dud." 496

The clock maker said, "Yes, that clock is good." 505

The woman said, "Here. You may keep this clock. I can't 516
stand it." She tossed the clock down, and it broke into parts. 528

So the clock maker left with the parts of the clock. He said, 541
"That woman keeps dropping the clock. But I'll fix it for her 553
again." 554

[2]

1

reached ouch painted toad

outside shook beads found

2

already garden wants parts collar

bopped dent bent shake

3

gone doesn't opened orange haven't

girl weeds know suddenly antlers blip

yellow bleep busted finger broken

across took one alligator

4

An Alligator Clock

The clock maker had painted a clock orange. He had made 11
the deer yellow. He had fixed the deer so that it bobbed up and 25
down like a frog. When the clock maker took the clock to the 38
woman, the woman got very mad. She tossed the clock down. 49
The clock maker took the broken clock back to his shop. He 61
was going to fix it again. 67

He had just put his work bib on when his wife came in. She 81
said, "Did you just come in?" 87

"Yes," the clock maker said, "I can grin." And he did. 98

His wife shook her head. Then she said, "A little girl is 110
outside. She wants to know if she can pick weeds in your 122
garden." 123

[2]

The clock maker said, "There are no seeds in my garden. 134
The plants are just getting buds. They won't have seeds before 145
the end of summer." 149

"Not seeds," his wife said. "Weeds. The girl wants to pick 160
weeds." 161

"Why does she want to lick weeds?" the clock maker asked. 172

His wife was getting mad. She said, "I will tell her that she 185
can pick weeds. If she does a good job, I will pay her ten 199
dollars." 200

"That's fine," the clock maker said. "But you don't have to 211
holler." 212

[1]

His wife walked from the room. Then the old clock maker 223
wiped his hands on his bib. "Time to go to work," he said. 236

He grabbed the broken deer clock and began to set it on his 249
work table when, suddenly, "bam." He dropped the clock. That 259
bent the yellow deer and made a dent in the side of the clock. 273
And the bell did not work. It went, "blip, bleep." 283

"Oh, my," the old man said. "Now I have a big job." He went 297
to the bin. He picked up a string of beads. "Good," he said. "I 311
can string these beads over the side of the clock. The beads will 324
hide the dent in the side." 330

[1]

Then the clock maker looked for a good deer in his bin. But 343
every deer was broken or bent. "Well, well," he said. The clock 355
maker rubbed his big bib. Then he said, "I may have a good 368
clock under the bin." 372

So the old clock maker looked under the bin. He came up 384
with a dusty old clock. He said, "This clock is busted, but I 397
think it is the clock I need." 404

The clock maker began to shake the dust from the clock 415
when the clock door opened and out came an alligator. It ran 427
across the front of the clock and bit the clock maker's finger. 439

[1]

The clock maker said, "Ouch! This clock doesn't have a deer 450
in it. It has an alligator." 456

The old man sat down and began to think. "How will I fix 469
that deer clock?" he said to himself. Then he jumped up and 481
said, "I've got it. I will fix the alligator so that it looks like a 496
deer. I will put antlers on it." 503

The clock maker reached inside the clock and grabbed the 513
alligator. He got some yellow paint and dabbed the paint on 524
the alligator. "Not bad," said the old clock maker. "That 534
alligator looks more like a deer already." 541

[1]

Then the clock maker took the antlers from the broken deer 552
and stuck them on the alligator. "Good," the clock maker said. 563
Then he slapped the alligator into the deer clock. He set the 575
hands of the clock at three o'clock. 582

Suddenly the bell went, "blub, blub." At the same time, the 593
alligator came out. It bobbed up and down like a frog. It bit the 607
old clock maker's finger. Then it ducked inside the clock. 617

The old man said, "That clock looks just fine now. The 628
woman will never know that I made another deer from this 639
clock. She will be glad to pay eleven dollars to get this fine 652
clock back." 654

So the old clock maker took the clock to the woman. 665

[2]

Lesson 55

1

ar

A	B
arm	are
part	yard
hard	garden
farm	barking

2

branch around jailer while

sounded toad cleaned sailing

scream shout horned beads told

3

birds first girl third roof stayed

bobbed blow wanted door buy

shape I've they've busted frog

dusty took antlers rapped

eleven garden already

4

The Clock in the Tree

The clock maker had taken an alligator from a dusty old 11
clock and had slapped it into the deer clock. The alligator was 23
yellow, and it had antlers. The old man said, "This clock looks 35
just like it did before." 40

So the clock maker took the clock to the woman. The clock 52
maker rapped on her door. The woman came to the door. 63

"What do you want?" she said. 69
"Here it is," the clock maker said. He held up the alligator 81
clock. "This clock is fixed up as good as ever." 91
[1]

The woman looked at the clock and said, "Oh, no. I don't want 104
to buy dusty clocks with beads on them. I had a good clock, 117
and you busted that clock. Now you are selling old junk clocks." 129
"Yes," the old clock maker said. "It looks just as good as 141
ever. Here, hold it while I set the hands." 150
Before the woman was able to back away, the clock maker 161
handed her the clock and began to set the hands. As soon as 174
the hands were set for five o'clock, the clock made a loud 186
sound. "Blip, blop," sounded the bell. 192
[1]

And here came the alligator. It bobbed up and down. It 203
bobbed this way and that way. It ran around the front of the 216
clock. Then it bit the woman's finger. 223
"Ouch!" yelled the woman. She dropped the clock. The 232
alligator grabbed her foot. The paint on the alligator was wet, 243
and now the woman had a big yellow spot on her foot. 255
Now the alligator began to bite the woman's leg. "Ouch, ouch," 266
the woman yelled. "What is that thing? It looks like a horned toad." 279
"Stop dropping that clock," the old man said. "You will 289
make more dents in it." 294
[2]

The woman yelled, "Make that horned toad stop biting me, 304
or I will bust that clock." 310
"Yes," the clock maker said, "there was some dust on the 321
clock, but I cleaned it up." 327
The alligator kept biting the woman's leg, so the woman 337

stepped on the clock. “Bing, bong, dong,” went the bell. Beads 348
went sailing this way and that. Then the alligator was still. The 360
woman said, “Get that clock out of here.” 368

“Yes, it’s a fine deer,” the clock maker said. “But I think you 381
bent the clock out of shape when you stepped on it.” 392

[1]

The woman yelled, “I don’t want that clock. Take it and get 404
out of here.” 407

The clock maker said, “Yes, I like that deer, too. But you 419
don’t have to shout. Pay me the eleven dollars, and I’ll be on 432
my way this day.” 436

“I’ll pay you this,” the woman said. She picked up the clock 448
and tossed it into a tree. It stuck on a branch. A little yellow 462
bird came and sat on the alligator’s antlers. Another bird came 473
and sat on the hour hand. 479

“Look at that,” the woman said. “Those birds like that 489
clock. They think it is a bird’s nest.” 497

The clock maker said, “Yes, it is the best. I just hope those 510
birds can tell time.” 514

[2]

The woman said, “For some time, I’ve wanted to get those 525
birds into my tree, but this is the first time they’ve come to the 539
tree. Thank you. How can I pay you for that?” 549

“Hand me eleven dollars, and I’ll be on my way this day,” the 562
clock maker said. So the woman gave the clock maker eleven 573
dollars, and the clock maker went home. 580

The woman stayed in her yard and looked at the birds. The 592
birds sat on the alligator. And when the wind began to blow, 604
the alligator bobbed up and down like a frog. 613

[1]

Lesson 56

1

ar

A	B
start	sharp
smart	barking
cart	hard
farmer	army

2

jailer scream outside chest years

pounded goat brains

shouted helper stuck

3

two nurse window around anything leave

room hospital want girl taking

what's doctor ready pretty because

fakes suddenly smiled trick

else floor snapping growled foxy

4

The Con Man Acts Like a Dog

When we left the con man, he was in the hospital. He had 13
told the cops and the jailer that he was sick. He really wasn't 26
sick. He was just playing sick. But the cop took him to the 39
hospital. The cop went up to a nurse and said, "Nurse, I have a 53
sick man. He needs help." 58

Lesson
56

The nurse said, "We will fix him up fast." She had the con 71
man sit on a cart. Then she took the con man to a room. 85
As soon as she left the room, the con man darted for the 98
door. He peeked outside. But the cop was standing near the 109
door. "Nuts," the con man said. "I will try the window." 120
[1]

He darted to the window. He grabbed the handles and 130
opened it wide. Then he looked out. There were bars on the 142
window. "Nuts," the con man said. 148
He sat on the bed and said to himself, "I must think of a trick 163
that will get me out of here." Suddenly he jumped up. "I've got 176
it," he yelled. Then he began to bark like a dog. He had a plan. 191
The nurse came running in. "What's that barking?" she asked. 201
The con man got down on the floor and growled at her. 213
"Rrrrr." Then he began snapping his teeth. 220
"Oh!" she screamed. "This man has gone mad." 228
[1]

The cop ran in. The con man barked at him. The cop said, "I 242
think this man is ready for the rest home. He is not well." 255
Three people came in and grabbed the con man. They took 266
him to a bus. The bus took him to the rest home. The con man 281
smiled to himself on the way to the rest home. He said to 294
himself, "My plan is working. They will take me to the rest 306
home. When I get there, I will tell the doctors that I feel better. 320
They will let me leave the home. I am very, very smart." 332
When the bus got to the rest home, the people led the con 345
man into a big room. Then a doctor came in. 355
[2]

A woman said, “Here he is, Doc. He thinks he’s a dog.” 367
The doctor said, “Thank you. We will give him the best of help.” 380
The three people left, and as soon as they did, the con man 393
said, “Doctor, I feel better now. I don’t think I’m a dog any 406
more. Why don’t you let me go home?” 414
The doctor said, “So you don’t feel like a dog. What do you 427
feel like?” 429
The con man said, “I feel like a con man.” 439
So the doctor said, “You think you’re a con man, do you?” 451
She began taking notes on her pad. 458
“Yes,” the con man said. “I think I’m a con man because I 471
am a con man.” 475

[2]

“I see,” the doctor said, and she took more notes. “When did 487
you start feeling like a con man?” 494
The con man was starting to get mad. “I’ve felt like a con 507
man for years and years.” 512
The doctor said, “Did you feel like a con man before you felt 525
like a dog?” 528
“Yes, I am a con man,” the con man said. 538
The doctor said, “Have you ever felt like anything else—a 549
goat or a farmer?” 553
“Look,” the con man said. “I never think I’m anything but a 565
con man. I out fox people. That’s what I do.” 575
“You feel pretty foxy, do you?” the doctor asked. 584
“Yes,” the con man said. He stuck out his chest. “I am the 597
king fox.” 599
The doctor called for two helpers. She said, “Lock this man 610
up. He thinks he’s a fox now.” 617

[2]

Lesson 57

1

pounded march brains heave charge

found garden easy around whatever

2

sir private squad charge remember

President foxy muttered okay Washington

3

escaped smiled maybe wait

window along helpers mean

our outside ground hadn't

people walked talk guy

two nurse want came odd

4

The Con Man Meets the President

The con man had told the doctor that he was very foxy. The 13
doctor had two helpers lock up the con man. The doctor said, 25
"That man thinks he's a fox now." 32

So the helpers took the con man to a little room at the far 46
end of the yard. They said, "You will like this room. You will 59
have a good time." 63

The con man said, "I am too smart for you. I will get out of 78
this room before the sun sets." 84

But the sun set, and the con man hadn't found a way to get 98
out of the room. He pounded on the floor. He tried to get out 112
the window. But the window had bars on it. And the bars did 125
not bend. 127

[2]

At last, the con man sat down on the bed. He said, “I will 141
have to think with my brains. There must be some way to get 154
out of here.” 157

Somebody said, “It is easy to get out of here.” 167

The con man looked around the room, but he did not see 179
anybody. The con man said, “Maybe I am out of it. I am 192
hearing people talk.” 195

Just then the con man saw a foot under the bed. The con 208
man grabbed the foot and gave it a heave. Out came a man. He 222
was smiling. He said, “Hello. My name is President 231
Washington. I am the father of our country.” 239

[1]

The con man said, “You seem really odd. I do not want to 252
share this room with you.” 257

The man stood up. He said, “If you keep talking like that, 269
you will end up in front of a firing squad.” 279

“Stop it,” the con man said. “You are not President 289
Washington, and there are no firing squads around here.” 298

The man said, “If you are going to be mean, I won’t tell you 312
how to get out of this room.” The man walked to the far side of 327
the room. 329

[1]

The con man said, “Okay, I won’t make fun of you if you tell 343
me how to leave this room.” 349

The man walked back and stared at the con man. Then he 361
said, “The best way to leave this room is to open the door and 375
walk out. Ho, ho.” 379

The con man said, “That’s not very funny, president.” 388

The man said, “But wait. I was just kidding you. There is a 401
way to leave this room. Here’s how it works: You hide under 413

the bed with me. When the helpers come into the room, they look around, and they don't see anybody. They say, 'We had better go for help.' They leave the door open, and they run from the room. Then we get out from under the bed, and we run outside."

[2]

The con man smiled. He said, "That is a fine plan."

The man said, "But remember, the plan is mine. Mine. And I am the president. So I will be in charge when we escape from this room."

The con man was getting mad, but he said to himself, "I must play along with this guy."

So the con man said, "Okay, you are in charge. I will do whatever you say."

"Good," the man said. "You may be a private in my army."

"No," the con man said. "I don't want to be a private."

[1]

The president jumped up and down on the bed. Then he started to scream. He yelled, "I won't let you leave this room if you won't be a private in my army."

"Okay, okay," the con man said. "I'll be a private."

The man said, "That's better. Now start to march, private."

The con man muttered to himself, but he began to march. He marched and marched and marched. Then the president said, "Now remember, private, when we make our escape, I am in charge. You must do everything I say."

"Yes, sir," the con man said.

[1]

1

wheat shouted alarm whispered

yard without nearby eaten mar hush

darted wait sneeze orders loose

2

love quick right who check

peeked cakes pressed while button

3

don't wants foot because

talking take tried tired

front escaped show rest

private across sir grove

hiding yum remember fool

4

A Foxy Escape—Part 1

The con man was in a room with a man who said that he was 15
President Washington. President Washington said that he was in 24
charge of their escape. The con man was just a private in his army. 38

The next day, the president said, "Soon they will come around 49
to feed us. When we hear them at the door, we will zip under the 64
bed. And we will wait without making a sound. Remember to do 76
everything I say, because I don't want anything to mar my plans." 88

"Yes, sir," the con man said. He was very tired. He had 100
marched and marched. He had taken lots of orders from the 111
president. 112

[1]

Just then, there was a sound outside the door. "Quick," the 123
president said. "Dart under the bed. And don't let your feet show." 135

The con man darted under the bed. The president darted 145
under the bed. Then the president whispered, "There is dust 155
under this bed, and dust makes me sneeze." 163

The con man whispered, "Don't sneeze." 169

"Hush up, private," whispered the president. 175

The door opened. The con man peeked out and saw two legs 187
walking across the room. Then he saw two more. "Where are 198
they?" a man asked. 202

"Hee, hee," the president whispered. "I can fool them every 212
time." 213

[1]

A woman said, "We had better sound the alarm. It looks as 225
if they escaped." 228

The first man said, "But how did they get loose? There is no 241
way out of this room." 246

"I don't know," the woman said. "But they are not here. I'll 258
sound the alarm. You check around the yard. Maybe they are 269
hiding nearby." 271

The con man saw the legs leave the room. "Hee, hee," the 283
president said. He slipped out from under the bed. So did the 295
con man. 297

Then the president ran to the table. The helpers had left food 309
on the table. The president said, "Oh, boy! Wheat cakes. I just 321
love wheat cakes. Yum, yum." 326

[1]

"Come on," the con man said. "We don't have time to eat 338
now. We must escape." 342

"Private," the president said, "sit down and eat your wheat 352
cakes. And if you don't do it right now, I won't let you have any 367
butter for your wheat cakes." 372

The con man said, "But, president, sir, the helpers will be 383
back soon. We must leave." 388

"No, private," said the president. "They won't be back for a 399
while. And you will see them coming, because you will be 410
standing near the door as you eat your wheat cakes. And you 422
will be keeping a sharp look out." 429

"Yes, sir," the con man said. He took his plate of wheat 441
cakes and stood near the door. 447

[2]

The con man had just begun to eat when the president said, 459
"Now we must go." 463

The con man said, "But I just started to eat." 473

"You are a very slow eater, private," the president said. "I 484
have just eaten three plates of wheat cakes." 492

So the con man dropped his plate. Then he began to run 504
with the president. They ran across the yard. They ran to the 516
front gate. The gate was locked. 522

"Hide in that grove of trees," the president said. So the con 534
man ducked into the grove of trees. 541

[1]

The president said, "Now I will go out and get the man to 554
open the gate for us." 559
"That man won't open the gate. He won't let us just walk out 572
of here." 574
"Private, hush up." 577
The president walked from the grove. He walked up to the 588
gate. He stuck his foot in the gate. Then he began to scream, 601
"Oh, my foot. It is stuck in the gate. Open the gate quickly." 614
The man who ran the gate pressed the button, and the gate 626
opened. Then the president began to yell. "Is there anybody 636
around here who can help me get my foot loose? Is there 648
anybody hiding in a grove of trees?" 655
The con man said, "That's me. He wants me to come out and 668
help him." 670
"I'll be right there," the con man shouted. 678

[2]

Lesson 59

1

oul could would should

couldn't wouldn't

2

nearest started loudly white shouted

steered please tooted main shack

3

full major bridal jogged green some

can't right they'll idea waved

spray hotel stared yokels jacket

company follow skipped two first

steered grove love quick

4

A Foxy Escape—Part 2

The con man ran from the grove of trees. He jogged up to 13
the president. The president smiled and said, "You see, private, 23
the gate is open. And we are free. Let's run down that road 36
before these yokels come after us." 42

So the con man and the president ran down the road. The 54
people from the rest home ran up to the gate. They said to the 68
gate man, "Did you open the gate and let those men escape?" 80

"Yes, I did," the gate man said. "But the first man had his 93
foot stuck in the gate. He was in pain." 102

"You yokel," the people said. Six people began to run after 113
the con man and the president. 119

[1]

Lesson 59

"I'm getting tired," the con man said. "Let's stop and rest." 130
"Hush up, private," the president said. "You'll never become 139
a major thinking the way you do." 146
"I don't want to become a major," the con man said. "I just 159
want to get out of here." 165
"Then do what I say," the president shouted. "We're going 175
back to the rest home. Follow me." 182
"What?" the con man asked. "We can't go back. They'll get us." 194
"No, no," the president said. "They don't think that we will go 206
back. That is the last spot they will look. Just do as I say, private." 221
[1]

So the president and the con man began to sneak back to the 234
gate. The gate was open, and the gate man was looking the 246
other way. So the con man and the president skipped by him. 258
They went to a shack near the grove of trees. 268
In the shack were white jackets. The president handed a 278
jacket to the con man. He said, "Private, slip into this jacket. 290
Then they will think that you work here." 298
When the con man and the president were dressed in white 309
jackets, they left the shack. The president led the way to the 321
main office. He walked up to the woman and said, "We have a 334
lead on those two men who escaped. We need a car to get 347
them. They are at a farm not far down the lane." 358
[2]

The woman said, "Take the green car in front of the office." 370
So the con man and the president got in the green car. The 383
president said, "You must drive. I am the president, and presidents 394
don't drive cars. They have privates who drive for them." 404
"Yes, sir," the con man said. He started the car and went 416
down the lane to the gate. The gate man waved at them and 429

opened the gate. The car went down the road. It went past the people who were looking for the con man and the president. The con man tooted the horn. The people waved at the car.
[1]

The con man steered the car to the nearest town. Then the president said, “Stop in front of the best hotel in this town. I am tired of driving. I must rest.”

“But—” the con man started to say.

“Hush up, private.”

“Yes, sir.”

So the con man stopped the car in front of the best hotel. The president smiled. He said, “It is a good thing we have these white jackets.” The president got out and walked up to the man at the desk. The president said very loudly, “We are from the bug company. You called us about the bugs you have in this hotel.”

“Shhhhhh,” the man at the desk said. “Don’t talk so loudly.”
[1]

The president said, “The man who called us said the bridal rooms are full of bugs. Show me to the bridal rooms.”

“Yes, yes,” the man said. “But don’t talk about bugs so loudly. I don’t want any people to hear that we have bugs in this hotel.”

“Private!” the president shouted. “Come in here and get to work.”

So the con man came running into the hotel. And the desk man took the president and the con man to the bridal rooms. The president said, “This looks very bad. We will have to spray this room. You can’t come in here for 24 hours.”

“Yes, yes,” the desk man said. “But please don’t talk about bugs.”
[2]

Lesson 60

1 **oul** would could shouldn't

2 alarm whiskers charge leave

ordered sneak lunch while about

3 curls high right remember

suddenly nobody give wig

idea blinked rapped first

bride bridal company buzz

closet mirror sweets full

rolled enemy attacking love

snoring pretty shaved chair

4

The Con Man Becomes a Bride

The president and the con man were in the bridal rooms of 12
the big hotel. The president had told the man at the desk that 25
he and the con man were from the bug company. The president 37
had said that somebody called about the bugs in the bridal 48
rooms. 49

The president said, "This is the life." He sat down on the 61
bed. "I need something to eat, private. Go down to the dining 73
room and get a big lunch for us. Charge it to the room." 86

The con man said, "But I'm not—" 93

"Hush up, private," the president yelled. "If you want to stay 104
in this army, you must remember that I am in charge." 115
"Yes, sir," the con man said. 121

[2]

The con man went down to the dining room and ordered a 133
big lunch for two. "Charge it to the bridal rooms," he said. 145
Then he went back to the bridal rooms. The president was 156
sleeping on the bed. The con man said to himself, "I must get 169
away from this guy, but I need a plan." 178
He sat in a chair and began to think. The president was in 191
the bed, snoring and snoring. Then the con man jumped up. 202
"I've got a good idea," he said. 209

[1]

The con man ran to the closet. He found a bridal dress in the 223
closet. He said, "I will put this dress on. Then I will sneak from 237
this hotel. Nobody will think that I am a con man. They will 250
think that I am a bride." 256
So the con man slipped into the bridal dress. Then he shaved 268
his whiskers. He looked at himself in the mirror. 277
"My hair is not right," the con man said. He went back to 290
the closet and found a wig with big, black curls. 300

[1]

Just then the president rolled over in his sleep. He rolled 311
right off the side of the bed. When he hit the floor, he jumped 325
up. "Sound the alarm," he cried. "The enemy is attacking us." 336
Then the president saw the con man. He said, "Hello there. I 348
am President Washington. Who are you?" 354
The con man said in a high tone, "My name is Jane." 366

The president walked over to the con man. The president 377
said, "My, but your dress is fine. And your hair is very pretty." 390

The con man smiled and said, "Tee, hee." 398

[2]

Suddenly, somebody rapped on the door. "Come in," the 407
president said. 409

A woman came in with the lunch for two. She had 420
hamburgers, pickles, corn chips, and cake. 426

The president said to the woman, "Give yourself a tip of five 438
dollars. Just charge it to this room." 445

"Yes, sir," the woman said. She smiled and started to leave 455
the room. Then she stopped and said to the con man, "What a 469
sweet dress." 471

The con man said, "Buzz off." 477

The woman left, and the president said, "Let's have a bite to 489
eat, my dear." 492

The con man said, "Tee, hee." 498

So the con man and the president sat down to eat lunch in 511
the bridal room. 514

[2]

1

ir

A	B
bird	shirt
thirst	dirt
first	sir

2

beard trained should dash army

loudly leaving ordered buster

3

Valley Forge hamburgers junk

smell bride high please

sniffed ago air floor attack

isn't away main talking winked

enemy battle striped suddenly

money sorry behind we've

4

The Escape from the Hotel

The con man and the president were having lunch in the 11
bridal room. The president said, "This room is a mess. I 22
told that bum private to get lunch. But look at the junk he 35
ordered. Hamburgers and cake. The army just isn't what it 45
was years ago." 48

The con man said, "You are so right." 56

"Yes, my dear. Let me tell you about the battle that we had 69

some years back. The enemy army had us holed up in a spot 82
named Valley Forge. We were—" 87

Suddenly, the president stopped. He jumped up and sniffed 96
the air. "I smell the enemy," he said. "They are going to attack. 109
I know it. And I don't even have my army with me. Where is 123
that private?" 125

[2]

The president ran to the window and looked down at the 136
street. "There are cop cars down there. We must escape." 146

The president ran to the closet and came back with dress 157
pants and a striped coat. He slipped into them. Then he cut 169
some hair from the con man's wig and made a beard with it. He 183
stuck the beard on his chin. Then he grabbed a top hat from 196
the closet. 198

He looked at the con man and winked. "Don't think of me 210
as the president," he said. "Think of me as a dashing 221
man-about-town." 222

The con man said, "Well, let's dash, buster." 230

"Who said that?" the president asked. 236

"Who do you think, buster?" the con man said. 245

[2]

The president began to get red. 251

"Private," he yelled. "I don't think this is one bit funny. Now 263
let's get out of here before the cops get us and send us back to 278
that rest home." 281

The president and the con man went down to the main floor 293
of the hotel. But, just as they got there, the cops came in the 307
front door. The con man whispered, "We've had it now." 317

"Hush up, private," the president said. "Just stick with me." 327

[1]

The president walked over to the desk. "What kind of hotel 338
is this?" he said very loudly. 344

The man behind the desk blinked. "What is the matter?" he 355
asked. 356

"The matter? I'll tell you what's the matter. THERE ARE 366
BUGS IN OUR BRIDAL ROOMS. DO YOU THINK WE 375
WOULD STAY IN A HOTEL WITH BUGS?" 382

"Shhhhhhhhhhhh," the man said. "Don't say anything 389
about bugs." 391

"Don't say anything?" the president said. "I'll say 399
EVERYTHING. THERE ARE BUGS IN THIS HOTEL." 406

"Please, please," the man said. "We will be glad to give you 418
another room, any room you wish." 424

"No," the president said. "My bride and I are leaving. Give 435
me my money back." 439

[2]

The man behind the desk said, "Yes, sir. Just how much 450
money was that?" 453

"TWO HUNDRED DOLLARS," the president said, and he 461
winked at the con man. 466

Very quickly, the man gave the president two hundred 475
dollars. As he handed the money to the president, he said, "I'm 487
very sorry about this. And if there is—" 495

"Let's go, my dear," the president said to the con man. 506

He grabbed the con man's hand. In his other hand he held 518
two hundred dollars. The president and the con man walked 528
past the cops. They went out the front door. They got into a 541
cab, and they drove away. 546

[1]

Lesson 62

1

ir

A	B
third	girl
shirt	first
bird	dirt

2

igh

A	B
high	light
sigh	night
right	spotlight
fright	brightness

3

inches afraid marching

neared beach trench chill

couldn't bleet louder

4

A	B
every	everything
any	anybody
some	something
no	nobody
her	herself
day	daytime

5

patrol gasoline month

barracks millions difference

heard moved animals trumpet

coming brap wake drams brick

brabble bubbling seemed

remembered moon been

sky planet attacked ago

6

Jean on Patrol

The night was cool. Jean looked up at the five moons in the 13
night sky. "I will never feel at home on this planet," she said to 27
herself. She was on night patrol. Her job was to patrol a strip 40
that led from the beach of the red lake to the barracks. 52
Nobody liked night patrol, not with the drams. 60

The drams were little animals that came from the red lake. 71
They looked like grasshoppers, but they were bigger. About three 81
times a year, they came out of the lake. When they did, things 94
got very bad. They ate everything in their path. They ate wood 106
and bricks. They ate the yellow plants that lived on the planet. 118
[1]

Last year, they had eaten the barracks. Seven years before 128
that, they had attacked some of the women who didn't get out 140
of the barracks. Nobody could find a way to stop them. The 152
drams moved like a big army, with millions and millions of 163
drams marching and eating, marching and eating. 170

Jean had been on the planet for a little more than six months. She 184
had seen the drams before. One night, they had come from the lake 197
making that "bzzzzzz" that they make. Then they had made their 208
way up the beach to the barracks, eating everything in their way. 220
[1]

Then the drams had stopped, just before they reached the 230
barracks. They had stopped going "bzzzzzz." They had 238
stopped marching. They had been still for nearly an hour. The 249
women had run from the barracks. 255

Everybody watched the drams. But the drams seemed to be 265
sleeping. Then the drams marched back to the lake. They went 276

under water, and that was the last time anybody had seen them. 288
As Jean patrolled the strip to the beach, she kept thinking 299
about the drams. Why had they stopped the way they did? 310
What made them stop? And when were they coming back? 320

[1]

Jean began to think of the things that had happened the 331
night that the drams stopped near the barracks. It was a hot 343
night, but heat did not seem to make any difference to the 355
drams. Three years ago, the women had made a trench and 366
filled it with gasoline. They lit the gasoline, but it did not stop 379
the drams. Drams kept piling into the trench. When the trench 390
was filled with drams, more drams came—by the millions. 400
They went to the barracks and attacked the women. 409
Jean remembered that the night was bright when the drams 419
had stopped. But brightness hadn't stopped the drams in the 429
past. When the women had trained spotlights on the drams, 439
the light hadn't seemed to bother them. 446

[2]

There must have been something about that one night that 456
made the difference, but what was it? Jean remembered that 466
she had been on her way to the barracks when the drams 478
started coming from the lake. She remembered how the women 488
had yelled, "The drams! The drams! Let's get out of here." She 500
remembered how some women ran to the barracks and began 510
to wake up the other women. 516
Jean had been afraid. She had never seen anything like the 527
drams before. But they had stopped. And Jean kept thinking 537
that there was something that had made them stop. 546

[1]

As Jean neared the lake, she stopped and looked over the 557
water. It looked like glass. At night you couldn't see how red 569
the water was, but in the daytime the water was bright red— 581
nearly orange. 583

Jean felt a chill as she was standing near the shore of the 596
lake. It was a big lake. It was so big that Jean couldn't see the 611
other side. The brabble birds were not making their "brap, 621
brap." Everything was still. 625

Jean was ready to patrol the strip back to the barracks when, 637
suddenly, she heard something in the water. It was a bubbling 648
sound near the shore. It became louder and louder. And then 659
she saw them coming out of the water, going "bzzzzzz." 669

The drams. 671

[2]

Lesson 63

1

igh

A	B
bright	sight
fright	light
high	moonlight

2

clearly thousands first

flash couldn't breathing

started Carla

3

wall move few remember

guy other soon idea

month major blow

melted tried skipping

silent frozen shiny

barracks button moment

messed springs stared

stayed attacked gasoline

fifty patrol pressed

4

The Drams Attack

For a moment, Jean was frozen as she looked at the drams 12
coming from the lake. She could see them clearly in the 23
moonlight. They were shiny as they moved up the beach. 33

For a moment, Jean didn't remember that she was to signal 44
the barracks as soon as she spotted drams. She wanted to 55
run—run as fast as she could go. She wanted to run as far from 70
the drams as she could get. But she couldn't seem to move. She 83
stared at the drams as they came closer and closer. They were 95
only twenty feet from her now. 101

[1]

"Move. Get out of here," she said to herself. But her legs felt 114
as if they had melted. 119

Then Jean began to think. She reached for her signaler. She 130
pressed the button. Lights began to flash in the barracks. 140
Women began to yell, "The drams! The drams! Let's get out of 152
here." 153

And Jean began to run. Now her legs felt like springs. Did 165
she ever run! It was about three blocks from the beach to the 178
barracks, and Jean ran to the barracks so fast that she felt as if 192
she had run only twenty feet. 198

[1]

When she got to the barracks, she ran up to the major. Jean 211
was breathing very hard. "Major!" she said. "Major! Major!" 220

The major said, "Take it easy." 226

"Major," Jean said to her, "the drams are coming. They're 236
coming. They're coming up the beach, and we've got to stop 247
them. We've—" 249

"Take it easy," the major said. "Go stand with the women on the other side of the barracks. We'll take over. Just stay out of the way of the drams."

"Okay," Jean said, and she ran to the other side of the barracks near a grove of bleet trees. There were about fifty women standing there. One of them said, "Were you the one that spotted the drams?"

"Yes," Jean said. "They're coming! They're coming!" Jean's hands were shaking.

[1]

Another woman said, "Where is Carla? I haven't seen her."

Some of the women yelled, "Carla, where are you?" But Carla didn't call back.

"Is she in the barracks?" Jean asked.

"I don't know," one of the women said. "She sleeps like a log. Maybe she didn't hear the signal."

"I will go get her," Jean said.

"No," one of the women said. "You stay here. Don't go back into the barracks."

The women fell silent. Far off, Jean could hear the "bzzzzzz" of the drams. They were coming up the beach. Soon they would reach the barracks. If anybody was in those barracks, she would be attacked. If Carla was in the barracks—

[2]

Jean ran for the barracks. Some of the other women hollered, "Come back. You can't go in there."

But Jean kept running. She ran inside. "Carla, Carla," she yelled. "Carla, where are you?"

Jean ran to the far end of the barracks. Carla's bed was 487
messed up, and her trumpet was on a table next to the bed. But 501
Carla was not in her room. 507

"Carla!" Jean called. "Carla!" 511

[1]

Jean ran to some of the other rooms. Then she ran back to 524
Carla's room. Then, suddenly, a sound came from the other 534
end of the barracks. Crash! 539

Part of the wall fell down. Then another part fell down. The 551
"bzzzzzz" of the drams became very loud. Jean could see them 562
now—thousands of them, marching into the barracks. 570

"I've got to get out of here," she said to herself. "But I've got 584
to find Carla," she said. "I can't leave Carla here with the 596
drams coming." 598

Jean tried to think. Her legs wanted to run. But she kept 610
thinking of Carla. And the drams were coming closer and closer. 621

[2]

Lesson 64

1

al

A	B
all	almost
call	wall
fall	always

2

sight streaming sharp

cheek would right eaten

3

A	B
her	herself
spot	spotlight
out	outside

4

off find air asleep middle

idea move few tried

swung wiggled still floor

alive trying report brave

even dumb every patrol

cliff move turn

5

Trapped in the Barracks

The drams were at the other end of the barracks. They had 12
eaten the wall, and now they were streaming over the floor. 23
Jean was standing outside the door to Carla's room. Carla was 34
not in sight. Jean had to get out of the barracks before the 47
drams reached her. And she had to find Carla. The drams were 59
coming closer. The "bzzzzzz" was very loud. 66

Jean ran into Carla's room. She grabbed the trumpet from 76
Carla's table. "I can make a loud sound with this horn," Jean 88
said to herself. She took in a lot of air. Then she pressed the 102
trumpet to her lips. 106

"Brrrrroooooooooooo," went the horn. 110

[1]

Suddenly the floor shifted. A crash came from the middle of 121
the barracks. The drams were getting closer. "No time to blow 132
the horn again," Jean said to herself. "I must get out of here." 145

She ran from Carla's room. A mass of drams was on the 157
floor. Jean tried to run past them, but one dram got on her leg. 171
It bit a hole in her pants. Jean tried to slap it off, and she tried 187
to run at the same time. Another dram was on her back. 199

"Ow," Jean yelled. She slapped the dram, and it fell to the 211
floor. Five or six drams were on Jean now. One got on her 224
cheek and bit her. A sharp pain shot from her cheek. She hit 237
the dram, and it fell to the floor. 245

[2]

Now there was a mass of drams on her. They were on her 258
arms and her neck. They were on her legs and her back. She 271
wiggled and tried to shake them off, but they were biting her. 283

She yelled and kept running. She ran over piles of drams. 294
She fell into a hole that they had made in the floor. She got out 309
of the hole and began to run again. She swung her arms this 322
way and that way. And she ran. 329

She ran from the barracks. Then she ran to where the 340
women were standing. The women rushed up to her and began 351
to swat the drams that were on her. Jean was crying and 363
shaking. She couldn't stand still. 368

[1]

Two women held Jean while the others slapped the drams. 378
Then one woman said, "These drams are sleeping. Look at 388
them." 389

Jean looked. The woman was right. The drams were not 399
eating. They were not going "bzzzzzz." They were hanging on 409
to Jean, but they were very still. 416

The major ran up to Jean. She said, "What do you think 428
you're doing? You're lucky to be alive. What made you go into 440
the barracks?" 442

"I had to find Carla," Jean said. 449

The major said, "Carla is on patrol out near the cliffs. She's 461
not in camp." 464

[1]

Jean looked down. One of the women said, "But look at the 476
drams, major. They're asleep." 480

"Yes," another woman said. "Every dram is sleeping. They're 489
not marching. They're just sleeping." 494

The major shook her head. "If that doesn't beat all," she 505
said. "I wish I had some idea about what makes them sleep." 517
Then she patted Jean on the back. "You did a brave thing," she 530
said. "I'm going to have to report you for not following orders, 542
but you did a very brave thing in trying to save Carla." 554

Jean looked up and said, "Thank you." 561

The women looked at the sleeping drams. They had made a 572
big mess. They had eaten all the plants from the beach to the 585
barracks. They had eaten nearly all of the barracks, even the 596
windows. But now they were sleeping. 602

[2]

Suddenly, a woman yelled, "More drams are coming." Three 611
spotlights turned to the beach. Jean could see the drams. They 622
had just come from the water, and they were starting up the 634
beach. 635

The major said, "I wish I had some idea about how to stop 648
them. But I don't know where to begin." 656

Jean tried to think. "Think," she said to herself. "Something 666
made the drams go to sleep. Think about what happened. Think." 677
Jean was still shaking, but she began to think of everything that 689
had happened just before the drams went to sleep. 698

[1]

Lesson 65

1

al

A	B
all	almost
fall	calling
wall	always

2

night part streaming proud

breathed blushing would

3

beach marching pipe crash hour

pressed months deeply water forgot

forget blowing bitten funny blast

stunned again hungry hunger lined

buzzing their why find off

4

Stop the Drams

Jean was trying to think of everything that had happened just 11
before the drams went to sleep. She remembered how she had been 23
running with the drams biting her. She ran and fell into a hole in the 38
floor. She remembered getting out of the hole and running again. 49

But were the drams biting her then? "Think, think." 58

"No," Jean said to herself. "I don't remember being bitten 68
after I fell into the hole. Something must have happened before 79
I fell into the hole." 84

Jean tried to think of everything that happened before she 94

fell into the hole. She looked at the beach. More drams were 106
marching closer to the barracks. They were marching over the 116
sleeping drams. “Bzzzzzzzzzzz.” 119

[2]

“Think, Jean. Think.” 122
“I was running from Carla’s room,” Jean said. “My running 132
couldn’t make the drams go to sleep. It must have been something 144
that happened before I ran. What did I do? What did I do?” 157
The drams were very close to the barracks now. “Bzzzzzzzzzzz.” 167
Jean started to rub her cheek. She saw that she was still holding 180
Carla’s trumpet. “That’s funny,” she said to herself. “I forgot that I 192
still had it. I must have held on to it when I ran from the barracks.” 208
Some of the drams were streaming into the barracks now. 218
“The horn,” Jean said. “I gave a blast on Carla’s horn. Maybe 230
that’s what stopped them.” 234

[1]

Jean breathed in deeply. Again she pressed the horn to her 245
lips. The horn let out a big blast. “Brrrroooooooo.” The drams 256
kept coming. 258
Part of the floor in the barracks gave way with a crash. Jean 271
shook her head. “The horn doesn’t work,” she said. “I have to 283
keep on thinking. I have to—” 289
Just then a woman yelled, “Look, the drams have stopped. 299
They’re sleeping.” 301
“The horn did it,” Jean yelled. “The horn stopped them.” 311
Some women began to slap Jean on the back. 320

[1]

“Good job,” one of the women said. “What made you think 331
the horn would stop them?” 336
“I don’t know,” Jean said. “I just kept thinking of everything 347

that happened before they went to sleep." 354
After about an hour passed, the drams began to move again. 365
But they didn't buzz or eat. They went back into the lake. 377
Now the women had a way to stop the drams, but they didn't 390
know why the trumpet worked. Three months passed before 399
the major told them why the trumpet worked the way it did. 411

[1]

"Thanks to Jean," the major said, "we know why the drams 422
come out of the water. They are hungry. They are hungry for 434
sound. They can't hear the kind of buzzing sound they hunger 445
for when they are under water. So they come out of the water 458
and buzz. They buzz until they have their fill of the sound. 470
Then they go back to the water. 477
"The sound of the horn gives them their fill of sound very 489
fast. It stuns them. When they are stunned, they seem to be 501
sleeping. After they wake up, they go back to the water. 512
"They don't come out for another three months or so." 522

[1]

One of the women said, "Does that mean that we can stop 534
them just by blowing horns when they come out of the water?" 546
"We can do better than that," the major said. "We can pipe 558
sound into the lake. We can keep them from getting hungry for 570
sound. If they don't get hungry for sound, they won't leave the lake." 583
The women smiled and looked at each other. Jean was 593
thinking, "Now night patrol won't be so bad." 601
Then the major said, "I would like to thank the woman who 613
showed us how to stop the drams—Jean Parker." 622
Jean could feel her cheeks blushing. But she was very 632
proud—very proud. 635

[2]